FINANCE IN EASTERN EUROPE

ABOUT THE AUTHORS

Karin Corner is a lecturer at Huddersfield Polytechnic. She specialises in the economics of Hungary and is the author of an article on *Lessons from Liberalization in Hungary.*

Bill Forsyth has taught at the Universities of Glasgow, Aberdeen and (since 1988) York. His principal interests are European and international economic history. He is currently preparing a book on the rise and fall of the DDR.

David Gowland is a lecturer in economics at the University of York. He previously worked at the Bank of England and as an adviser on financial and monetary policy to the Policy Unit, 10 Downing Street. His publications include *The Regulation of Financial Markets,* Edward Elgar (1990).

Wieslaw Kalinowski is currently Vice President of the Board, Bank Handlowy in Warsaw. He was formerly head of the monetary policy division (as Vice President) of the National Bank of Poland.

Katrina Ott is a journalist, an academic (University of Zagreb) and a policy adviser to the Croatian Minister of Finance.

Zbig Polanski works in the Institute of Monetary Research in the National Bank of Poland. In 1990–91 he was a visting Fellow at the University of Maryland. His publications include *Inflation and the Monetary System in Poland in the 1980s.*

Wieslaw Zoltkowski is a member of the monetary policy division, National Bank of Poland.

FINANCE IN EASTERN EUROPE

Edited by
D.H. Gowland

Dartmouth

Aldershot • Brookfield • Hong Kong • Singapore • Sydney

332.0947
© D.H. Gowland 1992   *F491*

Published by
Dartmouth Publishing Company Limited
Gower House
Croft Road
Aldershot
Hants GU11 3HR

Dartmouth Publishing Company Limited
Distributed in the United States by
Ashgate Publishing Company
Old Post Road
Brookfield
Vermont 05036
USA

A CIP catalogue record for this book is available from the British Library and the US Library of Congress

Printed and bound in Great Britain by
Billing and Sons Ltd, Worcester

ISBN 185521 251 x

Laserset by Computype Manuscript Services, Standard House, 49 Lawrence Street, York

Contents

List of tables

Introduction

ed.   Eastern Europe

P 34
P 21

The basic justification for this book can be stated in syllogistic form:

1. The governments of eastern europe are endeavouring to create a market economy.
2. A financial sector is both essential and vital to the functioning of a market economy. Critics and defenders of capitalism alike can agree on this, if on very little else.

Thus it follows that:

3. The most crucial task facing the reformers in eastern europe is to create an efficient, properly functioning financial system. Moreover, it can be argued that failure to achieve or even attempt this was the main reason for the failure of past reform efforts, notably in Hungary, Poland and Yugoslavia.

The purpose of this volume is to analyse the role of the financial system in four economies: Hungary, Poland, Yugoslavia and the former German Democratic Republic (DDR). They have been selected because in these economies and these economies alone, a major attempt has been made at marketisation. In the DDR this took the form of its absorption into the

1

German Federal Republic. In the other three, there were attempts at reform from the 1960s onwards. Hence, this book can look at the role of the financial system in a Stalinist economy, during the half-hearted reform of the later Communist period and in the attempts of the new post-Communist governments.

The first chapter (Gowland) is somewhat self-indulgent in that I have allowed myself the luxury of generalisation. The purpose of this chapter is to highlight what seemed to me to be the key issues developed in subsequent chapters. My perspective is unashamedly that of a western economist. This seems to provide some valuable insights. For example, Polanski (Chapter 6) describes recent macroeconomic policy in Poland. His account can be paraphrased as follows:

> the Polish authorities sought to control the financial system by means of credit ceilings. They found these unsatisfactory and were forced to replace them by reliance upon interest rates. Throughout the period, the authorities faced a worsening trade-off between the need to combat inflation and the desire to pursue a policy conducive to growth. In the end a new government decided that a drastic counter-inflationary policy was necessary. This worked and indeed, seemed to promote efficiency in certain sectors of the economy. Nevertheless, there was a terrible price to pay in terms of unemployment.

The above would be as accurate a description of the UK economy from 1952-83 as it is of the Polish economy. However, in Poland the events took less than 30 months instead of more than 30 years in the UK. Indeed, this is a general conclusion from my first chapter. There is frequently little difference conceptually between the problems faced in the OECD and in eastern europe. What is different is their extremity. The problems are far greater, events occur far quicker and all the policy choices are far starker.

Chapter 2 (Forsyth) presents an analysis of events in the DDR, concluding with its effective absorption by the GFR into a United Germany. Ott (Chapter 3) presents a fascinating account of events in Yugoslavia. She enjoys the advantage of being one of the key reformers, occupying a vital role in the Croatian Ministry of Finance. Chapter 4 (Corner) analyses the reasons for the failure of the Kadar reforms in

Hungary and considers whether the post-Communist attempts will be any more successful. Kalinowski and Zoltowski describe the introduction of a western-style monetary system from the perspective of the Polish Central Bank. The final chapter (Polanski, from the Research Institute of the same institution) complements this with a wide-ranging analysis of the problems faced by all the post-communist economies. He goes on to document and justify his conclusions with reference to the extraordinary recent history of Poland.

This book can be read as a coherent integrated study. Some key issues are highlighted in Chapter 1. Chapter 2 explains the role of a financial system in a Stalinist economy. All the satellite states shared a common structure, notably a monobank. The essential feature of a monobank is that it combines the role of central bank with that of commercial bank. The basic defects of the command economy emerge from the analysis in this chapter. Reform attempts are described in Chapter 3 but it is fair to concede that the reforms of the 1960s, 1970s and 1980s failed because the basic "socialist" system remained intact. Hence root and branch reform was necessary. This involved the creation of fundamental capitalist infra-structure, especially a capital market (Chapter 4) and a monetary system (Chapter 5). Chapter 6 describes the birth pangs of the switch to capitalism and synthesises the preceding analysis. However one can also view the book as an analysis of the same problem from different aspects. Ott writes with the commitment, even passion, of a participant. The Polish authors present the pragmatic realism one expects of central bankers. Forsyth has the incisive power of a historian and Corner the analytical skills of an economist.

Postscript

This book went to press in September 1991. Many of the articles in the Winter 1991 issue of the *Oxford Review of Economic Policy* (vol.7, no.4) would have been cited if it had been available in time. However, all of the economic analysis remains as relevant as when written despite the political and economic changes in eastern europe and what was once the USSR.

1 Finance and financial policy in eastern europe

D.H. Gowland

1.1 INTRODUCTION

The purpose of this chapter is to explore a number of issues in finance and financial policy in eastern europe. Many of these issues have emerged as a consequence of the collapse of the communist, command economies and the consequent attempt to create a market economy in their stead. Nevertheless, the reader may experience a feeling of *déjà vu*. Many of the issues that are now salient in eastern europe are ones that have been debated for decades in North America and western Europe. Kalinowski's and Zoltowski's comments on the inadequacies of the reserve base method of monetary control (see p.97), echo those of the Bank of England in rejecting this system or the Fed in trying to operate a means of control which is "as poor as that of a fisherman trying to reel in a tuna on a line that was alternatively as unyielding as an anchor chain and as elastic as a rubber band" to quote the classic aphorism[1] Indeed, in many cases the principal difference between the problems faced by the OECD economies and those of eastern europe is that the stakes are far higher in eastern europe. In both regions it is necessary to consider whether it is worth paying a price in terms of unemployment to eliminate inflation and structural inefficiency. However, in the west, the price may be 10-15 per cent unemployment, whereas in eastern europe, the price may well be 30-50 per cent unemployment.

It would be reassuring for the economist if the experience of the west offered guidelines for correct diagnosis and, if possible, prescription for the East. However, it may be that the reverse is true. Following the old scientific adage, experience at the extreme may offer guidance to those in more moderate circumstances, rather than the reverse. Whether or not this is true of the costs of inflation (Section 1.4) or the choice of optimal instruments (Section 1.5), it is certainly true of the institutional debate considered in Section 1.3. It is vital in eastern europe to consider whether markets should precede institutions or *vice versa*. It is equally crucial to determine which institution should be created first. Formal economic analysis as yet offers little guidance on these issues, yet they are simultaneously being faced in the European Community as it moves towards *1992*. The Hungarian solution, (see p.88ff), that institutions should be created prior to liberalisation is the same as the view put forward by the European Commission. The Polish view that market forces should be given their head and institutions allowed to emerge, is very similar to the British approach to this chicken-and-egg problem. Underpinning all of this is the $64,000 question: what should be the role of the financial system?

1.2 THE ROLE OF THE FINANCIAL SYSTEM IN EASTERN EUROPE

However much they may disagree about other issues, all of the many strands of economic thought that derive inspiration from Marx are agreed on one point: there is a fundamental contradiction between the interests of finance capitalism and those of industrial capitalism. It has frequently been argued that one of the major and longest-lasting problems of the UK and US economies is that the interests of industry, especially manufacturing, are subordinated to those of commerce, especially finance. It is both unnecessary and impossible to try to delineate the precise role of ideological as opposed to practical considerations in the creation of the Stalinist financial systems of eastern europe in the late 1940s and early 1950s: Keynes' point about the indirect influence of the academic scribbler on the practical man (Keynes, 1936, p.243) is highly apposite. The systems were created by self-avowed Marxists who had imbued Marxist writings for many years. Thus, it is not surprising that the financial systems created in Soviet satellite states of eastern europe bear many traces of the approach advocated by radical economic thinkers.

5

The basic argument of the Marxist school of economic analysis is that financial factors should never be allowed to determine economic decisions, especially those concerning investment. The argument is beguiling: if something is socially desirable, then it should not be frustrated by the whims of finance. The workings of the financial system should therefore be totally subordinate to those of the real system and should reflect the needs of the latter. This would be in contrast to the workings of the Anglo-Saxon economies, where the financial system is certainly autonomous and arguably in many instances, has been predominant. Hence the financial system in eastern europe prior to 1989 is usually regarded as unimportant. This conventional argument is advanced and documented in the chapters by Ott (3, concerning Yugoslavia), Corner (4 concerning Hungary), and Polanski (6, concerning Poland). They stress the significance of the absence of capital market discipline in their respective economies. Indeed, they attribute a considerable portion of the blame for the failure of the reforms of the 1970s and 1980s to failure to introduce this discipline. In particular, large state-owned enterprises were immune to financial constraints; they faced "soft budget constraints". In consequence, they pre-empted virtually all the available investment funds for unproductive projects. The heavy losses made by such industries created budgetary problems and placed such onerous burdens on the private sector that economic growth was frustrated. Parallel arguments have, of course, been frequently advanced in the UK, as a reason for the privatisation of publicly owned industries. A similar analysis is commonplace concerning, for example, the Italian economy. Indeed a similar point is made by Kornai (1986) himself regarding the provision of health care in western europe.

Forsyth (Chapter 2) enters an important caveat to this argument. He argues that the role of the financial system is very different in a Stalinist economy, but not necessarily less important. His argument is that the financial system was used as a replacement for the price mechanism to pass information to and co-ordinate economic activity. Obviously, the DDR system worked significantly less well than that in the FGR, but it did work. [2] It may be that there is no contradiction between Forsyth's proposition and the more orthodox one. It could be that the three chapters illustrate the danger and weaknesses of half-hearted reform. In both Yugoslavia and Hungary there was extensive if piecemeal economic reform from the 1960s and 1970s onwards. It may be that in consequence the Stalinist mechanism of control was destroyed, but that the reforms were not so fundamental that a replacement was devised. This would certainly fit in with Kornai's emphasis on the soft budget constraint (see p.81). His argument could be reinterpreted as a thesis that there was no adequate discipline on large state-owned industries in Hungary. There was neither the Stalinist mechanism described by Forsyth, destroyed in Hungary by reform, nor the Anglo-Saxon capital market mechanism. Such analysis is similar to that of the Polish authorities and their advisers who decided that a gradualist move towards a market system would not work. Instead, a "big bang" was necessary. This and its consequences are analysed in Chapters 5 and 6.

Forsyth's view may be part of a more wide-ranging thesis. It is clear that in the USA and UK, the financial and monetary system acts as a signalling device which ensures the co-ordination of economic activities. Forsyth's point is that one cannot divorce the financial system from the price mechanism that underlies it. Hence, the Anglo-Saxon financial system works in one way, whereas the Japanese system works in another because the underlying price mechanisms are different. Forsyth's analysis also emphasises that the financial system play different roles in different economies. This further exemplifies the Williamson (1988) approach as developed by Neave (1991). In Williamson's terminology, Forsyth demonstrates how the financial system can act as a governance mechanism without fulfilling the allocative function that is central to its role in an Anglo-Saxon economy.

1.3 INSTITUTIONAL STRUCTURES

Cambridge economists have frequently argued that all the interesting questions in economics are settled before one draws supply and demand curves. It is necessary to define a good. If I buy, for example, a video-recorder, then I assume that it will fulfil various functions. For example, I would feel cheated if it were impossible to change the tape. It is important to consider from whence I derived this opinion. It is even more important to determine who is responsible if the VCR does not work properly, or if it were to explode and damage my neighbour's house. All of these questions have received much greater attention from neo-classical economists in recent years. In part this has provided some answer to the post-Keynesian and Austrian critiques of their position. Economists like Roell (see Pagano and Roell (1992)) have analysed the micro-foundations of the structure of financial markets. The theory of regulation has also endeavoured to render endogenous the institutional structure that underlies markets. Nevertheless, both radical and neo-classical economists have done little more than focus on key issues in the area of institutional economics. The most important exception to this is in discussing the role of financial liberalisation in development,[3] a literature on which I draw later in this chapter, especially Stiglitz (1989). Much of this literature focuses on the debate between McKinnon and Shaw on the one hand and neo-structuralism on the other concerning the effect of financial liberalisation, Mohadiellin (1990). "Neo-structuralism" is not relevant in eastern europe as it concerns the implications of informal (black) loan and securities markets which did not exist in the satellite countries – McKinnon and Shaw argue that liberalisation will increase both the quantity of resources available for investment and the quality of their allocation: the classic liberal "invisible hand" argument accepted by all the authors of this book and assumed or stated in all chapters.

This *lacuna* is very unfortunate because a number of institutional questions are central to the problems of eastern europe. The governments of eastern europe have all asked their advisers about what priority to give to the creation of different facets of a capitalist system. Should priority be given to the development of a modern banking system? Alternatively, should priority be given to the creation of a well-functioning stock exchange? At least to the layman, these seem very pertinent questions.[4] The well-trained western economist would reflect that a stock exchange cannot operate without a clearing mechanism which in turn depends upon the existence of a banking system. On the other hand, the role of a banking system in choosing to whom to lend presupposes that the entrepreneurs have access to some source of equity finance. Unless ownership of the means of production is to be confined to former members of the *nomenklakutura*, then this requires a stock exchange. More generally, western economies have evolved as a seamless webb of institutions such that each institution depends on the existence of all of the rest. Hence, western advisers tend to say that one should endeavour to create all of the institutions of a capitalist economy simultaneously. This is certainly a logical answer but it is not necessarily the only one, nor a particularly useful one. Governments in post-communist countries do have to choose priorities and face the danger of trying to do too many things at once. McKinnon (1989, p.38) makes a very similar point:

8

we now recognise that our knowledge of how best to achieve financial liberalisation remains seriously incomplete. The *order* in which the monetary system is stabilised in comparison to the pace of deregulation of banks and other financial institutions must be more carefully considered than had previously been thought.

McKinnon's wording also implies the micro/macro choice, see below and Brabant (1990). Stiglitz (1989) argues that reformers should concentrate on the banking system and leave the securities market to a very late stage in the process of liberalisation. His analysis is based on the nature of market failure stemming from imperfect and assymetric information. He argues that venture-capital will not be available given all the problems he analyses, whereas debt capital via an intermediary may be; see also Lacker (1991) for the advantages of debt. Stiglitz concludes that foreign-owned banks may cut the Gordian knot. The Hungarian government believes that foreign participation in a securtites market may eliminate some of the problems analysed by Stiglitz (see p.90). Stiglitz concentrates on the mobilisation of domestic resources, the Hungarian government on foreign investment.

The importance of the correct ordering of a reform process is highlighted by one of the main problems of economic reform in eastern europe in both the 1970s and the 1990s. This is the danger of excessive concentration on commerce at the expense of industry. It is easy to see why this arises. Would-be entrepreneurs in eastern europe are faced with a shortage of capital and a fear that controls may be re-imposed. On the other hand, they are faced with excess demand for consumer goods. It is easy, profitable and, in fact, socially desirable to satisfy some of this demand. Hence, the rash of street sellers offering a wide range of imported consumer goods in Warsaw in 1990 or the much-vaunted restaurants in Budapest in the 1970s. Such activities offer a relatively high rate of return on capital. More importantly, they require relatively little capital and offer a quick pay-back period. On the other hand, it is extremely difficult to privatise heavy industry. Moreover, it is not a particularly attractive field for the entrepreneur. Hence, what is very likely is that a two-sector economy will emerge. One sector would be an inefficient publicly-owned manufacturing and heavy industrial sector. The other would be a vibrant, efficient, highly de-centralised service and commercial sector. The danger would be that the latter absorbed all of the developing nation's entrepreneurial talent and available capital. This problem of an unbalanced economy has been intensified by the high real interest rates introduced as part

9

of macroeconomic stabilisation policy. The public sector could become ever more stagnant and inefficient. Of course, to a much lesser extent, there are problems of over-concentration on commerce in the UK and USA, and of the burden of a backward public sector in Italy. However, the problem is far more intense and potentially dangerous in eastern europe.

The most obvious solution to this problem involves foreign ownership of the capital-intensive manufacturing and heavy industries. However, foreign investors are reluctant to invest on a sufficiently large-scale in eastern europe. Moreover, as exemplified by Poland, the political leaders of eastern europe share the attitudes of their western confrères to the question of foreign ownership. For a mixture of familiar reasons the, for example, Polish government has been reluctant to see excessive foreign ownership of its industry. On the other hand, the Hungarian and Czech governments have taken a much more welcoming attitude to foreign investment. Of course, their attitude might change if the scale of foreign investment were to increase substantially. This difference seems to lie at the heart of the most-debated difference between the Polish and Hungarian routes to a market economy. The Hungarian government has emphasised the importance of creating institutions, such as a stock exchange. The argument is that the existence of this infra-structure is a necessary pre-condition for the emergence of a capital market, in other words, of entrepreneurs seeking to raise funds. On the other hand, the Polish government has argued that it is necessary to create markets first by liberalisation and then to tailor institutions to their requirements. Ott's description (see p.68) of the pathetic state of the Serbian stock exchange exemplifies the rationale for the Polish approach. There is seemingly little point in creating an elaborate mechanism of a stock exchange complete with clearing house, unless there are some securities to trade. Otherwise, the reform is at best cosmetic and at worst risks diverting valuable resources and talent. On the other hand, budding entrepreneurs need a capital market if they are to be able to carry out their plans. It is possible that the nature of this divergence has been exaggerated. Kalinowski's and Zoltowski's chapter (5) describes the steps taken to create the institutional infrastructure of a money market in Poland. Nevertheless, the debate is both real and fascinating. It, as argued above, closely mirrors debates that take place within the *EC*. The UK government and Stock Exchange deny that it is necessary to create a European Stock Exchange. They argue that trading in equities from all 12 member states now takes place in London. So long as there are no official barriers, this

10

market is likely to grow naturally and become a fully-fledged European Stock Exchange. It will face competition from Frankfurt, Paris, Milan etc. Should London fail to provide an appropriate service to investors and those raising funds, then instead, a European Stock Exchange will emerge in one of the rival centres. Similarly, market forces will determine whether there should be one stock exchange or many, what settlement mechanism is most appropriate and so on. There may be a small role for the visible hand of government, but on the whole, it is best to allow market forces to operate unamelled. The European Commission's argument for positive regulation to create a European Stock Exchange mirrors the arguments of the Hungarian government. Hence, the issue of institutions or markets is not restricted to eastern europe.

In view, therefore, of the wide-ranging importance of the topic, it is regrettable that very little of the literature addresses it, still less, claims to resolve it. The standard neo-classical response is to argue that both are necessary. This would not be a very useful answer to say the government of the Ukraine if it were to ask its western advisers whether it should copy the example of Hungary or Poland. The point of this sermon is not to criticise but to argue for the importance of the case studies contained later in this volume. The experience of what was the *DDR* may be particularly relevant in that it inherited a complete institutional framework from what was the Federal Republic. The experience of Yugoslavia may also be apposite because it seems to have switched from a market approach in the 1970s to an institutional approach in the 1980s.

1.4 MACROECONOMIC POLICY

Polanski (Chapter 6) describes with apparent regret, the way in which micro-economic reform was subordinated to macroeconomic considerations in Poland. One line of argument is clear. A market system can only operate with a stable currency. Hence, a necessary pre-cursor to any successful economic reform is the elimination of inflation. This in return requires harsh economic medicine to stabilise the economy and provide the essential macroeconomic underpinning to macroeconomic success. This was the attitude of the Polish government in 1990. In many ways, its attitude and approach were very similar to those of Professor Erhard in West Germany after the Second World War. He chose to eliminate inflation by means of a currency reform of 1948. A hard-line anti-inflation policy remained central to his approach until his departure from office in 1965 and has been retained by his successors. This is echoed by the World Bank (1989) view for third world and post-communist economics:

> Reform should start by getting the fiscal deficit under control and establishing macroeconomic stability. The government should then scale down its directed credit programs and adjust the level and pattern of interest rates to bring them into line with inflation and other market forces.[5]

However, a counter-argument could be created based upon the experience of Japan. In post-war Japan little attempt was made to control inflation. Instead, priority was given to microeconomic considerations and to growth (the standard analysis of Japanese policy is Horicuchi (1984)). Other countries – Taiwan, South Korea, Singapore – have also assigned low priority to inflation in a transit phase whilst switching to being a high-growth economy. Low rates of inflation were in fact often achieved. However, they were not a policy priority. Horiuchi (1984) suggests that growth led to low inflation whereas the World Bank *et al* suggests the reverse. The debate between these two schools in an east european context is percieved by Brabant (1990); Kornai being taken to represent those who would give priority to growth and micro objectives, Portes to those who take the World Bank view. It is easy to see how the two objectives may conflict. To control inflation and stabilise the currency, the Polish government raised interest rates to about 6 per cent *per month* for investors in the state bank. Inflation was perhaps 2-3 per cent per month. Moreover, the zloty was successfully pegged to the dollar. It is impossible to work out the precise real rate of interest implied by this nominal rate, given the *ex-post* inflation rate and the foreign exchange policy. Nevertheless, it is a phenomenally high rate by any standards; contrast Horiuchi's (1984) emphasis on low interest rates. McKinnon (1984) cites a *positive* correlation between growth and real interest rates, an IMF house argument since about 1970. The casual connection is not established. Moreover third world experience may not be relevant in eastern europe. The direct and indirect effects of high real interest rates in Poland on investment were considerable. Moreover, they intensified the problem highlighted in the previous section, the bias towards commerce. Such interest rates would lead

12

entrepreneurs to give priority to activities that involved little capital and offered a short pay-back period.

Economists in the west have debated the relative importance of inflation and unemployment as evils for 70 years. Keynes (1923), Friedman (1974), Hayek (1972) and many lesser figures have all argued that inflation should be regarded as public enemy number one, and that priority should be given to its elimination.[6] The argument has been that inflation was not only undesirable in itself, but the main cause of unemployment. (Keynes may have modified this opinion later). In any case, most modern Keynesians have argued that inflaiton was undesirable and unpleasant, but might have to be tolerated as the price of keeping unemployment at an acceptable level. This proposition that inflation is often the lesser evil, has normally distinguished Keynesian from monetarist economists (see Mayer (1978)), though there are exceptions such as Dawson (1992). It is clear that the issue is central to the economic problems faced by all the countries of eastern europe including the Soviet Union and its successor states.

In constructing an active anti-inflation policy, the post-communist governments of eastern europe face a peculiarly difficult problem of excess effective demand. On the one hand, the citizens of these countries have faced chronic shortages for many years and have therefore a strong taste for a few basic consumer goods to alleviate their suffering. On the other hand, partly as a consequence of past excess demand, they have enormous liquid savings in various forms. In other words, they have the means necessary to render their tastes into effective demand. In such circumstances, economic liberalisation may cause problems. In countries as diverse as Chile and Egypt in the 1970s, the effects are well-documented and include balance of payments problems, distortion of the economy and social unrest.[7] The Polish response to this excess demand problem has been drastic deflation. In the DDR the excess demand has been satisfied from FGR sources. However, this has not been the end of the story. The excess demand now shows up as part of the vastly increased budget deficit of the unified German government. An aspect of this is a rather unusual but fascinating open-market operation. In effect the Bundesbank has been compelled to buy Ostmarks. Although the price was in excess of their market value, this is in some ways irrelevant. Any purchase of securities by a central bank must increase the money supply. Hence, the arguments between Chancellor Köhl and Bundesbank President Pöhl which ultimately led to the latter's resignation. Karl Pöhl seems to have believed that for reasons of political expediency, Chancellor Köhl had abandoned (West) Germany's hard-line commitment to an anti-inflation policy. The Hungarian and Yugoslav governments have made no real effort to eliminate this overhang of excess monetary demand. The reader is invited to read the relevant chapters below to see which approach seems preferable. One thing is incontravertible. The clash between long-run microeconomic and growth objectives on the one hand, and short-run counter-inflation policy is as central to the economics of post-communist Europe as it is in the OECD countries, Brabant (1990).

1.5 INSTRUMENTS OF FINANCIAL POLICY

Even if it were clear what the objectives of macroeconomic policy should be in eastern europe, the issue of the appropriate means would still remain. This issue has not been resolved in the OECD economies, so it is not surprising that it is not clear how it should be resolved in eastern europe. All of the standard problems re-emerge. For example, it is necessary to measure the money supply if one wishes to control it. In Poland, there has been a long debate concerning whether the appropriate measure should include or exclude dollar deposits held by Polish residents. Given that the dollar was used on a large scale as a medium of exchange in the 1980s, the answer is by no means clear. In 1990, the successful stabilisation of the Zloty and the payment of the high interest rates on Zloty deposits, led to a switch from dollars to Zlotys. Hence, the definition of the money supply which included dollars grew much less rapidly than that which excluded dollars. This could be interpreted as a switch from savings to transaction balances, and therefore a reason for monetary harshness, that is, the total of Zloty deposits is the relevant measure of money. Alternatively, it could be viewed as a switch from one form of transaction balances to another and totally irrelevant to future changes in inflation – that is an argument for a definition including dollars. Indeed, one might argue that the stabilisation of the Zloty should lower the velocity of circulation of money and so mean that the effective rate of monetary growth was below that of either statistical measure.

More generally, I must confess that as Editor, my initial reaction on reading Kalinowski's and Zoltowski's chapter was surprise that the problems on which they focus were so similar to those which appear in accounts of UK monetary policy. His *leitmotiv* is that text book methods of monetary control do not work in a liberalised environment. This echoes the conventional wisdom in the UK of controlling money in an era of financial invovation, Goodhart (1986, 1989, 1991).Polanski discusses the role of credit ceilings in Poland. As described in the Introduction, there are many parallels between his analysis and UK experience. In common with many other authors, I have frequently argued that the UK has yet to develop a viable and effective *modus operandi* of monetary control.[8] The EC is discussing the same issue as I write in the Inter-Governmental Conference on Monetary Union. Chapters 5 and 6 demonstrate that Poland, at least, faces identical problems.

To conclude, it seems that at least in some regards, the problems of eastern europe are those with which western economists should be familiar. However, in completely different institutional framework, they take on a fascinating new form: the subject of the rest of this book.

NOTES

1. See bank (1980) for the Bank of England view. The merits and disadvantages of the system are reviewed in Gowland (1982) Chapter 3. The quote is from Thomas Wagge, then Vice President of the Federal Reserve Bank of New York.
2. An interesting attempt to measure the DDR's economic success was made by in *Fortune* 3/12/1990. It is reproduced in *Economic Times* vol.1 no.2 (Fall 1991) p.20. He compares car ownership, ownership of consumer durables etc. in the DDR with the FGR.
3. The standard text in this area is Fry (1988) summarised in Fry (1988a). This is part of a special issue of the *Oxford Review of Economic Policy*, vol.5, no.4, devoted to an analysis of World Bank (1989) which also includes McKinnon (1989), a summary of his many contributions to the debates in this field, and Stiglitz (1989), refered to below.
4. The salience of the issue part became clear to me in discussions with (non-economist) employees of the Bank of Poland in Warsaw in June 1990. Belatedly, the similarity of this to the McKinnon point below in the development literature struck me.
5. This would seem to summarise accurately the views of the IMF and the Harvad School of advisers to the Polish Government, of which Sachs is the best known. I have not been able to find short quotes for their views.
6. For summaries of the debate see Sinclair (1987) p.21–3, Gowland (1990) Chapter 7 and Shone (1984) p.137.
7. For Egypt see Mohieldin (1991), for Chile see McKinnon (1989). Both include bibliographies.
8. For example in Gowland (1982).

2 The Socialist Financial System: the case of the DDR

W. Forsyth

2.1 INTRODUCTION

The financial system of the German Democratic Republic began to take shape in July 1945, four years before the state came into being. It was consolidated between 1948 and 1952 and, over the next four decades, it was central to the operation and development of the most successful economy in eastern europe. It disappeared overnight on 1 July 1990. The DDR survived it by three months.

Despite dogmatic reservations about the role of money in a socialist economy,[1] a financial system was essential to its operation. In the DDR that system became the single most important instrument for planning and guiding the economy and the most effective financial control mechanism in the communist bloc. The peculiar political circumstances behind the creation of the DDR meant that the system differed in form if not in operation from that in other communist states. Yet it was fatally flawed. The absence of market pricing was arguably the single most important cause of its failure here, as in the rest of eastern europe.

The effects of the basic design error introduced by a preference for non-market pricing were compensated for by over-organisation and obsessive bureaucratic control of a financial system whose jurisdiction extended far beyond the limits normal in the west. The drawbacks were hidden, until 1990, behind dubious statistics but also behind some

16

real macroeconomic progress. DDR figures indicated that, between 1950 and 1988, GNP per head grew faster than in any OECD country except Japan and by 1988, at around $9,000, was half that of the Federal Republic of Germany (FRG) and three-fifths higher than the average for eastern europe. Only in 1990 did German Economic Monetary and Social Union (GEMSU) reveal the true extent of systemic failure: unprofitable, overmanned enterprises with an obsolete capital base, poor quality product ranges and an economy kept afloat on a raft of subsidy which absorbed one third of the state budget. The performance – and survival – of the DDR economy over 40 years was in large part due to the financial system's ability to offset the growing economic difficulties created by an irrational and arbitrary pricing mechanism.

This paper will examine four themes: first, the growth and structure of the DDR financial system; secondly, its function in central planning in the DDR; thirdly its performance over the lifetime of the DDR and its impact on aggregate economic activity; and fourthly the consequences of the changes introduced by the monetary union of July 1990.

2.2 GROWTH AND STRUCTURE OF THE FINANCIAL SYSTEM

Growth

The financial system of the DDR was established after 1945 by the Soviet occupation authorities to achieve three tasks.[2] The first, and most immediate, was to gain full economic and political control in the Soviet Occupation Zone. The second, and most important, was to create a means of remitting war reparations. The third, incidental, task was to establish Soviet-style socialism. Given the order of priorities, the transformation of the prewar economy was more gradual than elsewhere in eastern europe. Public finances and zonal budgets were organised within weeks of the German surrender. Central planning was in place by 1950. The building of a state-run banking and credit system, however, was not completed until the later 1950s and the nationalisation of industry proceeded until 1972.

It was understandable that, having destroyed Nazism, the Soviets, like the western Allies, would seek to replace the political and social economy in their occupation zone with structures which resembled their own. Thus the organisation and operation of the state budget and the conduct and purpose of state fiscal and monetary policy in the DDR were similiar to those in the USSR and in the rest of eastern europe. However there were differences. The financial system was less monolithic and, as noted above, its restructuring was relatively slow. There were several reasons for this. Banking and insurance in those prewar areas of Germany which became the DDR had been extensive and highly sophisticated operations which served the most advanced regional economy in the country. Dismantling them would interfere with the extraction of reparations, which took precedence over all other ideological and practical considerations in Soviet policy towards postwar Germany. Moreover, the East German public in 1945 held a huge volume of war-inflated monetary assets in thousands of commercial and savings banks and insurance companies. Radical reform of the system would further alienate an already sullen population, encourage emigration across the open frontier to the western zones and complicate civil control. In addition, three other nations – the United States, Britain, and France – shared jurisdiction in Potsdam Germany. The USSR's scope for unilateral action in reforming its occupation zone was therefore considerably constrained.[3] Furthermore, in the postwar political flux in central Europe, there was a possibility that a combination of Soviet manoeuvring and popular elections could deliver the whole of Germany into Soviet control. Thus Soviet German policy in general and its attitude to the Soviet zone's financial structure in particular was tentative, provisional and contingent upon the resolution of the final political shape of Germany. This was evident by late 1945. All zonal financial institutions had been closed in April 1945. However, some parts, including some private banks, were later reopened despite German socialists' demands for complete nationalisation. Thus the socialisation of the East German financial system was not pre-planned. The changes between 1945 and 1948 were hesitant and tended to follow reforms in the western zones. Consolidation into a centralised financial system was not possible until Germany was financially and politically partitioned. That began with the currency reforms of 18-20 June 1948 in the three western zones and of 24-28 June 1948 in the Soviet zone. It was sealed by the creation of the Federal Republic of Germany on 2 May 1949 and of the German Democratic Republic on 7 October 1949.

Over the next 40 years the DDR's financial history fell into three distinct phases. The period from currency reform until 1963 was one of consolidation and centralisation. 1963-71 were years of decentralisation. 1972-1990 were characterised by a recentralisation of control.[4]

Between the currency reform and 1963, banking and credit were increasingly controlled by the political leadership of the Socialist Unity Party (SED) and merged with the centralised, physical planning of output which was characteristic of Soviet economic management. In July 1948 the German Note Issue Bank (Deutsche Notenbank – DNB) was created as a central agency of the Council of Ministers. With both central bank and commercial functions, it controlled not only the zonal banking system but was also a party organ for carrying out budget policy and for monitoring investment and business activity. In 1949 a centrally-planned and administered credit system was created which was integrated with the state budget. The budget itself was the financial counterpart of the physical output plan whose targets were the driving force behind all economic activity.

Throughout the 1950s, despite comprehensive and detailed control of output and finance, the DDR found it increasingly difficult, as did the USSR and other communist economies, to sustain growth and to raise economic efficiency. The reform experiment in the USSR under Khrushchev was therefore taken as sanction for a similar exercise in the DDR. The *New Economic System of Planning and Steering* (NES, 1963-67) and its successor, the *Economic System of Socialism* (ÖSS, 1967-71), led to greater decentralisation and to more emphasis on indirect monetary levers in directing economic activity.[5] The result was a functionally superior system; but central control and physical output targets were not abolished. In 1968 the DNB was restructured and became the State Bank of the DDR (Staatsbank der DDR). Its branches and those of several subordinate commercial banks became house banks allowing the SED leadership directly to control the activity of the state enterprises which produced four fifths of industrial output. At the same time new legislation made credit an active lever of state development policy. The banks were instructed to

'supply credits only on the basis of the efficiency of [their] investment... and in response to the input of [enterprises'] own resources'.[6] (Institute, p. 144)

The results of the experiment were unsatisfactory. The relinquishment of some financial and managerial control failed to yield the expected improvements in output and productivity. Furthermore, as the Czechoslovak experience in 1968 showed, economic experiment subverted communist power and invited Soviet intervention. Consequently, central financial control was reasserted in 1972, tightened further in 1982 and remained firmly in place until after the revolution of November 1989.

General

The structure of the DDR financial system reflected Soviet ideas on the purpose of money.[7] Money in the Soviet-style economy performed functions similar to those in market economies. It stored value, carried information, lubricated transactions and measured physical output and economic performance. However, it had an additional use. It was a tool for realising the demands of the Plan. Some of its forms nevertheless had side effects. Household savings and cash were largely outside state control and hence threatened the predictability of the Plan. Even business credits and monetary balances were only imperfectly controllable. Consequently the financial system in the DDR had a different form and function from that in the FRG.[8] There it was decentralised, democratically controlled and used to support market activity. In the DDR it was the central statement of the policy preferences of the Politburo of the SED, beyond parliamentary control and used to execute the Plan. In effect the financial system was the master of the economy, not its servant. By manipulating the monetary assets of the state, the banks, insurance companies and manufacturing enterprises and by controlling the financial flows amongst them through the budget and the State Bank, the political leadership were able to steer the DDR's economy to a degree unattainable in the west.

The state financial system in the DDR had two main components, one under central political control, the other decentralised. The main outlines are set out in Table 2.1.

Table 2.1: The structure of the DDR financial system[9]

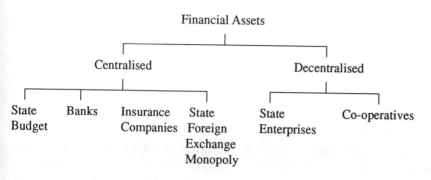

Source: Buck, (1985) p. 410.

In the DDR the financial system was primed by the redirection of a considerable part of national income through a range of production and consumption taxes and social security premiums into a number of centrally-controlled accounts. Of these the state budget was the most important for, through it, the definitive redistribution of national income occurred. As in the west it funded state activities; but, to a greater degree than in mixed economies, it provided much of the capital and operating revenues for the national economy. Through its control of the balances of the banks and insurance companies it also regulated all other important financial flows in the economy. Budgetary outlays directly affected the activities of nationalised industry and producer co-operatives and the level and direction of consumer demand. In 1988 budget revenues and outlays in the DDR each equalled national income. In the FRG the comparable figures were around 33 per cent.

The State Budget.[10]

Only limited comparisons are possible between DDR and western budgetary experience since the quality and extent of DDR data were poor and the nature and function of the budget were different. Moreover, the basis for taxation was dissimilar. Taxes were levied by economic and social group, only on the basis of taxable assets or of value added. In addition the state was not only the tax authority, but also the owner of the

21

national economy; so the distinction between taxes and levies on the earnings of DDR businesses was blurred. The extent of the state's economic influence was also, by western standards, exceptional. The state budget funded the administration, the social security system, much of the economic infrastructure, a considerable share of investment, a significant part of the activities of agriculture, industry and services, almost all public facilities and the mass social organisations such as the trade unions and the Free German Youth movement (FDJ). It also provided the heavy subsidies which kept basic consumer goods and services such as food, rent and travel cheap, and agriculture and industry solvent. It incorporated the tax and social security revenues of the central government and the budgets of all subordinate regional authorities and other state agencies, economic and non-economic alike. It was, thus, not only the state's revenue and expenditure account, as in the west. It was also the consolidated financial plan for all economic and most social activity, the financial counterpart of the national output plan. Like the latter it had the status of a law.

The preparation of the DDR's state budget plan (Table 2.2) clearly shows the extent and depth of central financial control, the tight timetabling and the rigid pattern of instructions and responses moving within the system. The grand Plan began in outline with the preferences of the Politburo. It was passed, through the Council of Ministers, to the State Plan Commission (Staatliche Plankommission) and to the Ministry of Finance for formulation and execution. A series of disaggregated draft plans were issued to Regional councils and these were further broken down into draft plans for lower level authorities and their subordinate enterprises. These lower levels then proposed modifications to the relevant drafts. The reasons were varied but the commonest was to bid for increased resources in order to ease their central task, that of fulfilling their part of the Plan. The modified draft plans were progressively consolidated at the different executive levels and returned to the central authorities. They, in turn, consolidated the counter bids into a modified draft plan which was sanctioned by the Council of Ministers and approved by the People's Chamber (Volkskammer). The Plan was next disaggregated into a series of fixed allocations for regional and local authorities and enterprises. These allocations were for precise purposes: for investment, to subsidise socially desirable production, to pay

Table 2.2: Preparation of the State Budget Plan

Administrative Level	Phase 1 Preparation of Draft Plan. Publication of Plan Tasks		Phase 2 Discussion and modification of draft Plan		Phase 3 Ratification. Distribution of Plan requirements	
	March	May	May	November	December	February
People's Chamber Council of Ministers State Plan Commission/ Ministry of Finance Other central authorities Subordinate enterprises Individual establishments	Proposed Plan			Draft Plan	Legislation	
Regional assembly Regional council Subordinate enterprise						
County assembly County council Subordinate enterprise						
Community assembly Community council Subordinate enterprise						

Source: Johannes Gurtz and Gotthold Kaltofen, *Der Staatshaushalt der DDR. Grundriss*, 2nd edn (Die Wirtschaft, East Berlin, 1982), p. 137

productivity bonuses; but all had the overriding task of funding the fulfilment of the mandatory material requirements of the national output plan. Although regional (Bezirkstage), county (Kreistage) and local assemblies (Gemeindevertretungen) approved the appropriate portions of the financial plan, there was, in fact, no effective external control. The Council of Ministers had the power to alter the budget after it was enacted. In the 1980s some two thirds of state revenues came from sources whose levels were not fixed by parliament.

As Table 2.3 shows, excluding social security receipts, nearly three quarters of all public revenues and expenditures passed through the central budget. In the FRG the corresponding figure was one third. Subordinate authorities had trivial revenue raising powers and little discretion in the use of the 2.5 per cent of income which they raised. The balance, subject to strict controls on its use, came from central transfers.

Table 2.3: State expenditures by administrative level, 1983

FRG			DDR		
	bn DM	%		bn M	%
Federal Government	247	32	Central government	137	72
States (Länder)	175	23	Regions (Bezirke) &		
Communes (Gemeinden)	73	9	local authorities	37	20
Social Security	277	36	Social Security	16	8
Total	772	100		190	100

Source: Bundesministerium für innerdeutsche Beziehungen, *Materialien.* Table 5.1-1, p. 551.

In addition to its greater centralisation, the purpose of the budget differed markedly from that in the FRG. It had an allocative role: to provide administration, law and order, defence, capital and social infrastructure. However, its main roles were redistributive – to allot national resources to uses required by the Plan – and directive – to monitor the execution of the Plan and, through the use of a complex system of taxes, credits and bonuses, to enforce compliance and to promote efficiency.

Until 1970 only aggregate revenue and expenditure data were published and no breakdown into components was available. Since then a more detailed picture has been available. The pattern is shown in Table 2.4.

Several features may be noted from the table. The first is the high level of direct taxation in the overall revenue account and the rapid growth of subsidy in the expenditure account. In 1988, direct taxation yielded 75 per cent of DDR state revenue as against 50 per cent in the FRG. Social security taxes provided only seven per cent of revenue, less than one fifth of the corresponding yield in the FRG. Subsidies were also vastly inflated by FRG standards. 20 per cent of expenditure in the 1970s, they were 35 per cent by 1988 (FRG under 5 per cent). As noted below, the level of subsidy was a direct consequence of the system of price formation in the DDR.

The second feature of the table is the different balance of burdens and benefits amongst different economic groupings. The tax burden fell on state production rather than on consumption with business and agriculture providing 95 per cent of all revenue. The comparable figure for the FRG was under 40 per cent. Payments to the state from these sectors were three and a half times greater than their receipts from it. All state sectors were subject to a range of taxes,[11] contributions and levies on capital (Produktionsfonds- and Handelsfondsabgabe), net profits (Nettogewinnabführung) and on individual products (Produktgebundene Abgaben) which were a large component of the producer price. From 1984 a 70 per cent payroll tax, disguised as a social fund levy (Beitrag für gesellschaftliche Fonds), added greatly to industrial costs. Taxes were also levied on the activities of banks and agricultural and craft co-operatives. In contrast to the large net business burden, households were net beneficiaries. Subsidies on households' goods and services were seven times greater than their income tax payments. The decline in private sector revenue after 1970 was due to the continued decline of independent activity in the economy.

A third feature of the budget was the rapid growth in unspecified revenues and expenditures. By 1988 13 per cent of revenues and 18 per cent of expenditures were unidentified. It is likely that the revenue

25

Table 2.4: State Revenues & Expenditures in the GDR, 1970–1988 (bn M)

	1970	1975	1980	1988
Total Revenues	70.6	114.7	160.7	269.7
Sources:				
Nationalised industry taxes, of which:	38.0	70.3	97.7	165.1
Production and trade fund levies	5.9	13.3	18.2	30.0
Net profit transfers	12.7	26.7	40.1	43.6
Product-related levies	19.4	30.3	39.3	43.1
Social fund contributions	–	–	–	35.2
Production co-operative taxes	3.1	2.6	3.1	5.0
Agricultural taxes	1.1	1.3	1.4	4.2
Private sector taxes	6.9	2.4	3.0	4.2
Income taxes	3.7	5.3	6.8	10.0
Social insurance payments	8.9	11.8	15.2	18.8
Revenue from state facilities	4.5	6.7	8.7	10.9
Transfers from bank profits	–	3.4	6.1	9.8
Other revenue	–	1.0	2.3	5.9
Unspecified revenues (residual)	4.4	9.9	29.3	35.8
Total Expenditures	70.0	114.2	160.3	269.5
Flows:				
Research	2.5	1.8	2.6	4.0
Investment	4.1	3.4	6.7	10.4
Transport	1.5	3.5	2.9	6.1
Subsidies, of which:	13.7	22.9	37.3	94.0
Industry	3.6	5.0	7.1	23.4
Agriculture	0.3	2.4	6.1	6.8
Consumer foodstuffs	4.8	7.2	7.8	32.9
Other consumer goods and public transport	1.5	3.4	8.0	16.9
Housing and rents	2.4	4.3	7.2	16.0
Grants to agriculture	2.3	0.6	2.4	1.2
Education and health	11.7	15.9	19.3	33.3
Social insurance transfers	15.9	21.4	29.4	36.3
Leisure and broadcasting	1.2	2.4	3.4	5.6
Administration	3.1	3.5	3.7	4.5
Defence, law and order	6.7	9.6	13.1	21.7
Other expenditure	–	1.6	2.2	3.8
Unspecified expenditures (residual)	8.2	27.6	38.2	48.1

Source: Vortmann, 'State budget', Table 18.2, p.149; *Statistisches Jahrbuch*, 1989.

figures represented further taxes on industry (for example penalty payments for the underfulfilment of Plan targets) and that the expenditure data contained subsidies for foreign trade and support for unprofitable enterprises.

Given the DDR's concern for innovation, efficiency and quality, it is significant that Table 2.4 shows research and investment expenditures growing more slowly than any sector except administration. However these figures are misleading since, over the period from the 1950s, the sourcing of investment shifted from the state budget to enterprise self-finance and bank credits. Before 1963 interest-free budget credits funded two-thirds of investment, enterprise funds one-fifth. By the 1980s budget grants accounted for only 15 per cent of gross investment, internal enterprise funding for 57 percent and bank credits the balance.

With the exception of the Social Fund Levy, enterprise taxes were allowable costs in the process of price formation in the DDR. Thus, in spite of low retail prices for most basics, the DDR consumer was the ultimate revenue pump for the state.

The Banking System

The banking system was the other main agency of financial and economic control used by the political leadership. It was highly centralised, hierarchical and rigidly controlled, as Table 2.5 indicates.

Although there was no Soviet-style state monobank, the bank structure of the DDR had one tier. Activity was divided amongst a number of banks with exclusive areas of competence whilst enterprises were required to hold accounts with one specified institution. Transit trade was controlled by the German Commercial Bank (DHB) whilst foreign trade was administered by the German Foreign Trade Bank (DABA). Agriculture and the food industry, artisanal industry and the railways were served by specialist banks. Households were served by a network of post office, savings and giro banks; but services and credit and interest rate policies were identical and centrally regulated.

The banking system was under the direct control of the State Bank of the DDR. This was not only the bank of issue and final settlement. It was also an agency of the ruling SED and an executive arm of the Plan. By the 1980s the State Bank had three functions beyond its conventional

27

Table 2.5: Structure of the Banking System of the GDR[12]

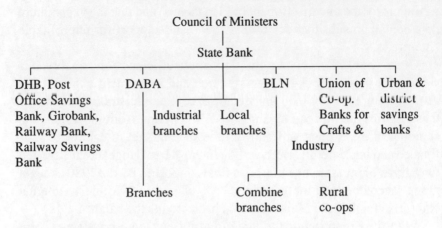

DHB	Deutsche Handelsbank (German Commercial Bank)
DABA	Deutsche Aussenhandelsbank (German Foreign Trade Bank)
BLN	Bank für Landwirtschaft und Nahrungsgüterwirtschaft (Bank for Agriculture and the Food Industry)

Source: Haase (1985), p.147.

central bank role. First, it prepared the array of monetary plans required to construct the national Financial Plan. Secondly, it supervised the adherence of banks, industrial combines and regional and local authorities to the instructions of the Plan. Thirdly, it conducted commercial banking. It had 15 regional boards, 41 industrial branches, 180 district and local branches and over 100 other branches and foreign exchange offices.

The banking system allowed the political leadership to transmit its orders to all levels of administration and economic enterprise and to have detailed control over their execution. In practice financial and economic control were imperfect since the information flows throughout the system were of low quality. The most important problem lay in the price system.

The Price System[13]

Like the budget and the banking system prices were tools of the Plan. They were measures of business activity. With taxes, interest rates, credit policy and physical balances, they were levers for implementing government wishes and managing economic activity. They were, themselves, objects of state planning. They were fixed by the Office of Prices (Amt für Preise beim Ministerrat) to optimise the goals of the Plan: maximal output, improved productivity, income redistribution, and the co-ordination of available supplies with pre-planned demand levels.

As in other east european economies before 1989, prices in the DDR were conveniences for national accounting rather than measures of relative scarcity or cost. The retail price (Einzelhandelsverkaufspreis – Table 2.6) consisted of a series of planned input costs and taxes, arbitrarily set to raise revenue or promote socially desirable output, not to stimulate efficiency. Their levels were not revealed and the final prices were only irregularly adjusted.

Table 2.6: Retail Price Formation in the GDR

	Production cost
+	Planned profits
=	Enterprise price
+	Product-related levy
(–	product-related subsidy)
=	Industry price
+	Wholesale trade margin
=	Wholesale price
+	Retail trade margin
=	Retail price

Sources: Bundesministerium für (subig) (1987), p.177.

This procedure had extensive and harmful effects throughout the economy. Prices were fixed and rigid. Until 1964 the ruling prices were those set in 1944. The result was a price structure which produced severe economic and financial distortions, provided increasingly meaningless information on costs and relative efficiencies and made planning more difficult. For nearly 40 years raw materials, energy, labour and basic consumer goods were underpriced, whilst consumer durables and non-essentials were overpriced. The further consequence was distorted production and consumption patterns. Capital goods and existing production methods took precedence over consumer durables and technically advanced processes. This led to a build-up of consumer purchasing power for which there was no countervailing flow of goods and services. Furthermore, growing labour shortages, falling domestic raw material production and rising world energy and import prices made periodic price revisions unavoidable. Adjustments in 1964-67 were sharp, unpopular and further complicated the work of the central planners. With no means of determining true resource costs, utility or scarcity, price revisions reduced but did not eliminate economic distortions. Price policy in the 1970s and 1980s concentrated on staged price reforms (in 1976-79 and 1979-84), adjusting product taxes, disguising the resultant inflation by massaging the retail price index and by reclassifying goods as new or improved products and raising their prices. The remaining imbalances were concealed by budget subsidies. These piecemeal reforms left planners operating with three sets of prices: revised prices for most goods, cost-related prices for others and arbitary prices for new or improved products.

2.3 FUNCTION AND PERFORMANCE OF THE FINANCIAL SYSTEM[14]

Function

In market economies the official and private components of the financial system have distinct roles. State financial policy is essentially directive and redistributive. It uses fiscal and monetary means for example to avoid or to correct for market failure, to stabilise economic activity, for regional restructuring and for income redistribution. Private sector banks and financial intermediaries, whilst subject to state regulation and responsive to state financial policies, are relatively free to fund the monetary needs of the state and of the dominant private sector. Their impact is determinable only *ex-post* through changes in the financial aggregates.

In the DDR the function of the financial system was different. Between 1945 and 1953 its role, increasingly, was to help create the centrally planned economy. Confiscatory taxes and discriminatory credit conditions were, along with nationalisation and the collectivisation of agriculture, part of a range of methods used to destroy private enterprise. Discrimination against the private sector continued up until the end of the republic. In 1988 private enterprise produced only 2.4 per cent of national industrial output, yet it generated 5.7 per cent of industrial tax revenues.

Beyond this, until 1963 the financial system's role was limited. Economic growth and stability were controlled by direct commands. Monetary policy was passive and credit policy was restricted to monitoring the distribution and use of capital and credit. Yet monetary control was comprehensive. Of ten central government agencies, four – the State Audit Office, the State Bank, the Price Office and the Central Investment Inspectorate were directly concerned with monetary matters. At combine and enterprise level two posts, those of chief accountant and director of the price division, had similar responsibilities.

By 1960 however, the DDR faced increasing economic problems. Growth was slowing and a labour supply crisis loomed. The lack of consumer goods and services, constant pressure on workers to raise output and the collectivisation of agriculture between 1952 and 1960 led, by 1961, to the flight of 2.7 million refugees, 15 per cent of the country's population, to the FRG. The building of the Berlin Wall in August 1961 stopped the loss of manpower, but 1950s-style planning could no longer raise the technical level and the efficiency of the economy. The New Economic System of Planning and Steering (NES) introduced indirect financial control and created a more important role for the financial system. Fixed assets were devalued, depreciation rates raised, industrial prices reformed and enterprise accounting procedures improved. Strategic planning remained with the state; but more decision-taking was devolved on enterprise directors. Credit and interest rate policies, used directly to raise output and efficiency and to reward good and to penalise unacceptable plan performance.

NES, not surprisingly, was unable to revive the exceptional growth of the 1950s. Between 1963 and 1970 national income grew officially at 6.5 per cent a year compared with 8.3 per cent a year between 1950 and 1963.

Capital efficiency improved, but at a rate one-third that of the FRG. Moreover NES merely increased economic confusion in a system which was neither fully controlled nor now entirely decentralised. Financial levers did, however, improve economic control and when, in the 1970s, central control was reasserted, they continued to play a significant role.

Some aims of financial policy in the DDR were the same as in the FRG: securing the stability of money as a unit of account, medium of exchange and store of value and aiding the full employment of labour and capital. However, policy had other aims which were either absent in the west or were private sector prerogatives. The most important were first, to regulate the the supply of money to the productive sectors to permit plan goals to be achieved and to adjust its flow to accord with the actual level of Plan attainment; secondly, to avoid cash flow and credit bottlenecks which could impede the attainment of Plan targets; and, thirdly, to increase the total money supply and volume of consumer credit in step with the real growth of the economy and the availability of consumer goods. The main instruments of financial policy were the central budget, and the State Bank-dominated banking system.

The Budget[15]

The budget's main function was to direct central revenues and expenditures to achieve the inputs and outputs specified by the Plan. Taxes were technically the fiscal obligations of the non-state economy and of the public. Other, larger, unrequited transfers were regarded as internal movements from one state sector (nationalised and co-operative enterprises) to another (the state budget). With direct control of all productive assets and with a pliant parliament, the central leadership had great fiscal freedom. The tax structure discriminated against industry and in favour of the consumer, against consumer durables and in favour of raw materials and basic household necessities, whilst the income tax code was biased against low income earners and in favour of young people and large families. Ultimately, however, the effective incidence of indirect and hidden taxation placed the main fiscal burden on the consumer. In 1988 70 per cent of industrial taxes were passed on to the public in higher industrial prices and taxes comprised 55 per cent of the final price for consumer durables and non-essentials. Thus, although the income tax and social insurance burden on earned income was less than that in the FRG, indirect taxation was significantly greater.

Taxes were levied to fund state consumption and expenditures. Along with other levies and payments, they were also used to raise efficiency. Thus taxes on fixed and circulating capital were designed to improve capital efficiency, whilst the social fund contribution was intended to release hoarded labour. The budget accounting methods, by tracking the flow of these funds through the system, recording the demand for supplementary funds and noting claims for efficiency bonuses, signalled the condition of the economy to the central authorities.

The Banking System[16]

The State Bank was the sole source of monetary creation: commercial banks had no autonomous power to do so. It issued 'emission directives' which limited the level and use of bank credit and it was empowered to siphon off commercial bank reserves in excess of those needed by the banks and their customers to fulfil their respective Plan obligations. It further manipulated monetary demand by setting interest rates and conditions for credit which served the Plan or an approved social purpose. The priorities of policy are clear from the interest rates current in the late 1980s. These are shown in Table 2.7.

The commercial banks regulated the supply of funds to the nationalised, co-operative, artisanal and private sectors of the economy. Through the legal obligation of enterprises to bank with a single, named bank and to settle transactions only through bank accounts, not in cash (Kontenführungspflicht), the commercial banks acted as agents of the state bank, minimising the use of cash in the system and even conducting transactions independently of the wishes of the account holder. In combines and large enterprises bank branches acted as house banks. The commercial banks also regulated the supply of funds to the public. They controlled consumer credit and, by using their controls on enterprise funds and credits, they could restrain unplanned pay rises. The sole significant task of the savings banks was to operate the interest-bearing demand deposits of the public and to discourage the use of cash, which was subject to household, not central, control and whose unpredictable use could disrupt the Plan.

Performance[17]

Between 1950 and the late 1980s, DDR national income rose nearly ninefold whilst material welfare reached the highest levels in eastern europe. By 1988 gross domestic product per head[18] (using questionable conversion rates) was more than twice that of the USSR and on a par with Greece. The DDR was one of the world's top twenty exporting nations.

Table 2.7: GDR Interest Rates in 1989 (per cent)

Nationalised enterprises	
Research & Development credits	3.8
Approved Plan credits	5.0
Unplanned credits for approved initiatives	5.0
Surcharge for bridging loans and unplanned credits	1.0 – 3.0
Penalty rate (e.g. on overdrafts)	12.0
Agriculture & food enterprises	
Investment credits	2.0 – 5.0
Surcharge for bridging loans and unplanned credits	1.0 – 3.0
Penalty rate	12.0
Home improvement loans	0.0 – 4.0
Consumer credits	
Young married couples	0.0
Large families	3.0
Basic rate (e.g. for consumer durables)	6.0
Household savings	3.25
Short-term deposits	1.0
Long-term deposits	2.0 – 4.0

Sources: Buck, (1985(c)), p. 1564f., Mayer & Thumann (1990), p.69

The performance of the financial sector in this achievement is difficult to assess since the relevant data were either uncollected, unpublished or of poor quality. By the 1980s an integrated system of direct and indirect steering mechanisms with a multitude of controls provided comprehensive regulation; but they generated limited efficiency gains. Moreover, the financial system was under increasing strain.[19] As the economy became more complex, physical output targets became less potent instruments of microeconomic control. Increasingly sophisticated monetary direction was needed. Financial planning, like physical planning, involved a huge output of reports, tabulations and projections for use by financial agencies themselves and by other parts of the planning and control apparatus. Much of the material was inconsistent or expressed in notional values and relativities which hindered the effective monitoring of the Plan. As trade grew, financial planning was further complicated by the need to take account of world price changes and the parities between the leading world currencies and the arbitrary values of Valuta Marks and Transfer Rubles in which DDR trade was measured.

2.4 MONETARY POLICY[20]

Monetary Policy

Over the 40 years of its existence the DDR appeared to follow sound monetary policies. The money supply increased in line with the Plan. The budget was in surplus. Internal prices and the (notional) external value of the Mark were stable. Yet at enterprise, bank and consumer levels effective monetary control was weak. Enterprises inflated their credit needs in order to increase resources and ease Plan fulfilment. Unplanned wage increases and bonuses were granted in order to hold on to scarce skills. Banks, in turn, were under State Bank pressure to minimise authorisations and to earmark credits for specific tasks. Enterprise directors responded by bypassing official channels, illegally reshuffling credits, withholding payments to suppliers and ignoring repayment deadlines. The results were first, chronic supply bottlenecks (which encouraged the hoarding of labour and stocks) and lags in commissioning new plant; secondly, a drain on the state budget for bridging finance and, thirdly, the introduction of ever tighter monetary controls to prevent these abuses. Together with the problem of unrealistic prices these activities made effective planning virtually impossible and the published balances and accounts a nonsense. Only the leadership's monopoly on financial flows and the limited impact of the world market on internal prices made the system operable. By the 1980s it was sustainable with increasing difficulty and only through increasing state subvention.

Monetary controls were also unable to limit household purchasing power or to control the public's use of cash holdings and savings. Between 1950 and 1988 cash in the economy rose fourfold; but, with full employment and an inadequate supply of acceptable goods and services, household savings rose 120-fold.[21] In 1985 household cash and savings exceeded 21,000 Marks per head, 120 per cent of net household income. Monetary reform in 1967 and frequent savings drives reduced cash hoards and made savings easier to control; but they did not permanently reduce the purchasing power overhanging the system.

Other policies also performed poorly. Budgetary policy had increasingly to compensate for price-induced economic distortions and to subsidise current output at the expense of investment and research. Fiscal policy was preoccupied with squeezing inefficiency and hoarded labour from the system and with steering current economic activity rather than with strategic planning. The results were the repeated changes in economic course noted earlier, continual unavailing efforts to improve the operation of the system, changes in the structure and management of enterprise and ceaseless exhortations to businesses and the labour force to raise productivity.

Price Policy[22]

Price policy also operated to facilitate the attainment of the Plan rather to achieve a rational allocation of output, to promote efficiency or to encourage innovation. Its effectiveness was nullified by the unrealistic level of planned prices, by the low quality of information which they yielded, by the chronic distortions which they introduced and by the state's refusal to allow bankruptcy to cull unviable firms. Price policy thus was confined to maintaining the convenience of fixed-price planning and the pretence of price stability. By 1988 many prices were still at their 1960 levels; but this was the result of the price freeze, the rigging of the Retail Price Index, the use of hidden subsidies and the diversion of repriced and sought-after goods to special retail outlets.

The policy of maintaining rigid and unreal prices frustrated the leadership's desire to economise on scarce resources whilst increasing the level and quality of output. Together with the extent of other financial controls and bureaucratic meddling, it also served further to blunt business effort.

2.5 GEMSU[23]

In 1989, on the occasion of the fortieth anniversary of the creation of the republic, the *Statistical Yearbook* of the DDR noted that

'the DDR reveals itself as a politically stable, economically efficient socialist state with a modern industry and agriculture and with a flourishing science and culture'.[24]

The Yearbook showed an economy achieving its Plan targets. Industrial production grew by 2.5 per cent. Yet, for the 1980s as a whole, excessively tight planning and chronic supply bottlenecks produced general under-performance. Labour and domestic raw materials became scarcer. Energy became dearer as COMECON prices moved nearer to world ones. Technical improvement was insufficient to compensate for these increases. The resource cost of exports also rose. In 1980 it took 2.40 Marks to buy 1 D-Mark of imports.[25] By 1988 it took on average 4.40 Marks. Increasing consumer complaints about the range, quality and reliability of supplies induced the government to increase imports and to pay for them by international borrowing at a time of rising world interest rates.

Until the end, although the political leadership experimented with systemic improvements,[26] it took an immense managerial effort just to keep the system functioning. At the enterprise level, for example, investment controls were relaxed in 1988; but enterprise directors' plans were still subject to external scrutiny, to unilateral interference from

37

government agencies and to local authorities' requests for more consumer output. Added to this were the daily problems of shortages and breaks in supply, the search for substitutes in the shadow economy and the constant need to provide performance indicators to higher authorities.

By the 1980s it was clear that, despite ceaseless state propaganda to the contrary, the DDR economic system repressed enterprise, efficiency, quality and innovation and ignored the consumer. The system supplied cheap basic goods and services, but little of quality and novelty. The system continued to operate, but only as an autarky. With the opening of the Austro-Hungarian frontier on 2 May 1989 a sequence of events began which culminated in the revolution of November 1989. Driven by growing anti-government demonstrations and by a flood of refugees (340,000 left the DDR in 1989, 2 per cent of the population) the political structure imploded. On 7 November the communist government resigned. A democratically-elected, non-communist administration finally took office on 18 March 1990. On 3 October the DDR became part of a united Germany within the EC. On 18 January 1991, after new elections, the first all-German government since 1945 was sworn in.

Parallel to this political process were moves designed to create a western market economy in East Germany. The economic base had to be privatised, economic decision-taking decentralised, and the financial system radically overhauled before the area could be integrated with the West German economy. On 18 January 1990 the two Germanies signed the State Treaty on German Economic Social and Monetary Union (GEMSU). Ratified in June 1990, it came into effect on 1 July 1990.

GEMSU, later consolidated by political unification, had profound financial effects for the DDR. Until 1990 the communist state owned all real assets but was a net debtor to the public who held the bulk of financial assets. These had been valued in distorted prices and denominated in a currency with no direct international exchange value. Integration required western financial institutions, rules and procedures and the conversion of Mark-denominated assets into D-Mark assets.

The first stage,[27] the recreation of a commercial financial structure, was initiated by the reform of the State Bank on 6 March 1990. This created a two-tier banking system similar to that already existing in West Germany. The State Bank retained its central banking role (until GEMSU); but its commercial activities were transferred to the newly-created German Credit Bank (Deutsche Kreditbank) whilst its Berlin office became the Berlin Municipal Bank (Berliner Stadtbank). Similarly, the central and branch operations of the BLN were divided into, respectively, the Berlin DDR Co-operative Bank (Genossenschaftsbank Berlin der DDR) and a series of rural co-operative banks. The savings banks were reorganised as public corporations, on West German lines.

Whilst institutional reforms were important in rebuilding commercial banking and insurance services, the rate at which existing Mark assets were converted to D-Mark assets was critical for economic activity. It affected not only the balance sheets of businesses and of the new regional governments but also business costs, prices and output, wages and employment and the success of the Treuhandanstalt, the trust agency set up to privatise 8,000 state companies.

On 1 July 1990 GEMSU came into force. The D-Mark became the common currency of the two states. The West German Bundesbank replaced the State Bank as the central bank of the DDR. West German systems of banking, taxation, welfare, wage bargaining, labour and property law replaced DDR statutes. Price controls were abolished after nearly 60 years. This amounted to

'the overnight replacement of the centralised command economy by the market economy'.[28]

On conversion day the DDR financial system was in credit. The main need was to establish a Mark – D-Mark conversion rate which maintained liquidity without bankrupting the state or state businesses and without unleashing excessive consumer spending.[29] Three conversion rates were applied:

1. 1M = 1DM for currency and deposits held by the East German public (up to certain limits prescribed for different age groups), wages salaries, rents and leases, bank equity and for trade balances with market economies.
2. 2M = 1DM for all other financial claims and liabilities, including trade balances with state trading companies, with the exception of
3. 3M = 1DM for Mark deposits placed after 1 January 1990.

GEMSU therefore significantly altered the pattern of assets and liabilities in East Germany. A consolidated national balance sheet for 1 July 1990 was not available at the time of writing; but the IMF has calculated one for the banking system for 30 May 1990. The main elements are reproduced in Table 2.8.

Table 2.8: Consolidated Balance Sheet of the GDR Banking System
(30 May 1990)

Assets	bn M	M/DM Rate	bn DM	Liabilities	bn M	M/DM Rate	bn DM
Domestic Credit	361.3	2.1	180.7	Domestic Credit	249.0	1.59	156.6
of which:				of which:			
Enterprise	231.7	2.0	115.8	Enterprise	57.0	2.05	27.8
Household	2.5	2.0	1.3	Household	182.1	1.48	123.4
Foreign Assets	45.0	1.24	36.3	Foreign Liabs.	56.1	1.0	55.6
Other Assets	4.2	1.1	2.6	Currency	13.6	2.0	6.8
Government				Other	30.6	1.13	27.0
credits[a]	36.1	–	–	Equity	23.4	1.0	23.4
				RIKOs[a]	96.4	–	–
	446.6	2.03	219.6		446.6	1.81	246.0
Equalisation							
fund			26.4				
Total	446.6	1.81	246.0		446.6	1.81	246.0

a. RIKOs (Richtungskoeffizienten) were shadow exchange rates which equalised domestic prices and the exchange rates used in foreign trade.A RIKO account, operated by the State Bank, reimbursed state exporters for exchange losses from the gains made by state importers. RIKOs were not converted, but 31.2 billion DM were credited to the government account to compensate. A further 4.9 billion DM were credited for the costs of currency creation in 1948.

Source: Schinasi, (1990), Table 1, p. 146.

With assets revalued at 2.03 to 1 and liabilities at 1.81 to 1.0, conversion left the DDR financial system insolvent. The solution was an Equalisation Fund (Ausgleichsfond), equivalent to 11 per cent of liabilities. The conversion rate had a significant effect on the balance of

40

assets and liabilities of the major economic groupings. It reduced household assets by more than liabilities and reduced, at one stroke, much of the cash overhang in the system. By wiping out state liabilities and creating a 36 billion DM credit, it left the state as a net creditor. Conversion at 1.0 to 1.0 also secured the the equity base of the banking system. Enterprises' bank assets were also converted more favourably than liabilities which marginally improved their credit position.

However conversion also exacerbated short-term adjustment problems. First, its overall impact on industry was negative. Conversion produced a portfolio of capital assets which exceeded corporate debt; but as Table 2.9 reveals, it significantly increased the debt burden.

Table 2.9: Conversion and Company Accounts (1988 data)

	bn M	bn DM
Net fixed capital assets	940	230
Obligations: gross	−230	−115
financial assets	60	30
Obligations: net	−170	−85
Debt − asset ratio	0.18	0.37

Source: Economic Bulletin, 27, 9 (November 1990), p.3f.

Thus the value of company fixed assets fell by three-quarters, obligations fell by one-half and the debt-asset ratio, which had been in line with that in the FRG, doubled. The position worsened after unification. High levels of obsolescence and unacceptable environmental operating standards meant that up to one half of the capital stock would have to be scrapped, thereby further increasing the debt burden. The introduction of market rates for corporate debt further weakened company balance sheets.

Wage conversion also had damaging effects on the viability of East German firms. East German wages were converted at 1.0 to 1.0, well above the labour market's clearing rate. Since wages and labour productivity were both about one-third of those in the FRG, this should have posed no particular cost constraint. After GEMSU however, East German industrial wages rose sharply and by October 1990 had risen 16 per cent whilst output per worker remained unchanged. By 1991 East German wages were half of those in the FRG. The reasons were various: compensation for the loss of subsidies and for higher taxes; a demand for equal pay for what was perceived as equal effort; little managerial resistance to union pay demands; a desire to stop the migration of labour; and a strategy to maximise the wage levels on which generous unemployment benefits were calculated. The results were a sharp rise in labour costs and a fierce cost-price squeeze. After GEMSU East German firms were unable to cover short-term costs and many assets had only scrap or site value. With low quality collateral and poor trading prospects, enterprises faced serious difficulties in raising capital and credit. This further complicated the task of the Treuhand in disposing of the state enterprises in its charge.

Secondly, conversion produced a switch in consumer behaviour. Provided with convertible DM, East German consumers switched their demand from domestic products to higher quality, more attractive West German goods. Thus, whilst demand remained high, domestic producers, hampered by sharply increased debt and soaring costs, found their internal markets collapsing.

Thirdly, producers' external markets also deteriorated abruptly. Their export subsidies ceased. Soviet and eastern europe demand contracted in the aftermath of the revolutions and market reforms in those areas.

Despite cutting prices – by July 1990 producer prices were about half those of 1989 – East German enterprises could not compete in price, quality or design in western markets. In only one sector, energy, did short-run costs justify foreign trade. Overall the domestic resource cost of earning one DM through foreign trade had improved since GEMSU; but was still 1.84 DM.[30] For the Wartburg car company and for the Pentacon optical company, the equivalent figures were, respectively, 1.89 DM and 7.00 DM. Wartburg was closed in 1991. The steel industry, which in 1988 had had an output of eight million tons, had a capital stock so obsolete, output of such low quality and was so poorly managed that it was beyond redemption. It was closed with loss the of 140,000 jobs

The combination of revaluation and the cost problems noted above produced instant and widespread insolvency and a collapse in output which was exacerbated by the continued emigration of key workers to West Germany. Between 1989 and late 1991 real GDP fell by 32 percent[31]. By January 1991 net manufacturing output was one-third of that in January 1990. By the fourth quarter of 1991, two million had been lost, 12 per cent of the labour force were unemployed and 23 per cent were on short time. The end of job guarantees and salary support in July 1991 for half a million civil servants will produce an additional 200,000 redundancies. With tax revenues of only 150 DM per head, one ninth of the West German levels, and with mounting mounting social security costs, the 'new federal states' have current fiscal deficits equivalent to 30 per cent of regional GDP. They are currently kept afloat by large West German transfers.

2.6 CONCLUSION

GEMSU swept away the East German financial system. It transferred fiscal and monetary policy to West Germany and price and wage determination to the market. It solved East Germany's problem of inadequate supply; but it revealed an obsolete, unviable economic base, a distorted and meaningless price and wage structure and a heavy foreign debt. The inevitable, painful readjustment has left the new states in serious financial difficulties and the Federal government with a budget deficit which has tripled to 65 billion DM since early 1990, despite a 17 billion rise in tax revenue. One quarter of the budget in 1991 is earmarked for supporting the financial and economic restructuring of East Germany.

Monetary policy is not a major problem for the federal authorities since the DDR economy was small relative to the FRG economy. It added ten per cent to the FRG's GNP. Currency conversion added only 13 per cent to West German M3. Although it contributed to an inflation rate currently at 4 per cent, conversion and unification costs have had no effect on the DM exchange rate against the SDR.

Fiscal policy is, however, a major concern for the federal authorities. Estimates of borrowing for 1990 and 1991 of 126 and 189 billion DM are respectively 40 and 70 per cent above original estimates and represent 6 to 8 per cent of West German GDP. Of the supplementary budgets and transfer payments, currently running at 75 billion DM, half are required for unemployment and pension fund support in the new states.

In late 1991 East German stabilisation is dependent on growing transfers from West Germany. Economic decline continues, although consumer expenditure remains strong, sustained by higher pay, West German transfers and by the drawing down of household savings. However this demand has stimulated West German activity. Only in services, which in the short run can not be imported, has there been significant growth in East Germany. Recent estimates suggest that the rate of decline is slowing and that it will be halted in 1992 and reversed in 1993. However, unless East Germans are prepared to accept lower standards of income and welfare until their economic performance is on a par with West Germany's, the roles of the German financial system in general and the fiscal system in particular will be dominated by the need to make considerable net transfers to East Germany for the next 10 to 15 years.

NOTES

1. For a discussion see Garvy (1966). A Soviet view is provided by Levchuk (1979). The most useful German sources are Gutmann (1983), Buck (1985b) and Haffner (1987). The standard GDR text is Autorenkollektiv (1981). The definitive guide to the terminology of the GDR financial system is Autorenkollektiv (1978-1980). Wilczynski (1981) is a less comprehensive but more user friendly alternative.
2. The best sources in English are Nettl (1977), Phillips (1986) and Sandford (1983). The background to postwar Soviet policy is dealt with in Fischer (1975, esp. Ch.5). The definitive study of the transformation of the banking system is Deckers (1974) whilst the emergence and development of the economic system is examined in Thalheim (1987)
3. Deckers (1974, pp.122f); Hedtkamp (1965).
4. Haase (1985a, esp. pp.143-146); Deckers (1974, pp.13-121).
5. Pohl (1977, pp.39-43); Melzer (1987). For perceptive studies of the use of monetary and fiscal 'levers' in the GDR economy during and after NES, see Knauff (1983, esp. pp.167-185), Thieme (1983, esp, pp. 298-321), Thieme (1987a) and Thieme (1987b).
6. Haase (1985a, pp.144).
7. Autorenkollektiv (1981); Buck (1985a); Garvy (1966); Hedtkamp (1987); Kaemmel (1958).
8. For a comparison between the systems in the FRG and GDR, see Hedtkamp (1987).

9. Buck (1985a); Buck (1976). See also 'Finanzkontrolle und Finanzrevision', 'Finanzorgane'and Finanzplanung und Finanzberichterstattung' in Zimmermann (1985, pp.390-400).

10. The best studies of the nature and function of the budget are Pohl (1977, pp.178-198), Haase (1982) and Vortmann (1989a, 1989b. Schnitzer (1972) is useful for the 1950s and 1960s but has otherwise been superseded. For a general discussion of fiscal systems see Musgrave (1969). Excellent studies in German are Leptin (1977); Bundesministerium (1987, pp.547-595); Gurtz and Kaltofen (1982); Haase (1985b); Haase (1985c), and Hedtkamp (1987, esp. pp.198-204).

11. For brief outline of the basic taxes see especially Bundesministerium (1987, pp.554f) and Buck (1985c, pp.1315-1322). Their effect on industry in the 1980s is discussed in Haustein (1989).

12. Haase (1985a, pp.146ff); Pohl (1977, pp.65-68); Schnitzer (1972, pp.307-329).

13. See 'Preise' in Autorenkollektiv (1979); Bundesministerium (1979, pp.506-519); Melzer (1985); Melzer (1989).

14. Hartwig and Thieme (1985); Pohl (1977, pp.59-72); Hamel (1983); Buck (1985a); Deutsches Institut (1984, pp.102-117); Thalheim et al (1987).

15. Haase (1985b, p.1280f).

16. Bolz (1985); Buck (1976); Buck (1985c).

17. Cornelsen (1989a, 1989b, 1989c); Wilkens (1981); Rytlewski (1985); Statistisches Jahrbuch der Deutschen Demokratischen Republik (Annual). The last issue of the Jahrbuch was for 1989. It can be supplemented by Statistisches Bundesamt (1990).

18. For problems of measuring GDR aggregates see Collier (1985) and Marer (1983).

19. Cornelsen et al (1989); Melzer (1982); Melzer and Stahnke (1986); Economic Bulletin (1986);

20. Buck (1985b); Hartwig and Thieme (1985).

21. Schwartau and Vortmann (1989); Bundesministerium (1987, pp.482- 546).

22. Melzer (1985, p.1043).

23. Lipschitz (1990); Mayer and Thumann (1990); Thumann (1990); Economic Bulletin (1989a); Economic Bulletin (1989b).

24. Statistisches Jahrbuch (1989, p.iii). For West German views of the GDR economy at the time of the revolution see Economic Bulletin (1990a, 1990b) and Deutsches Institut (1991).

25. Akerlof et al (1991); Collier and Siebert (1991); Siebert (1991)

26. Köhler (1989); Schilar (1989).

27. Schinasi et al (1990, esp. pp.151-154); Thumann (1990, esp. pp.160-163).

28. Economic Bulletin (1990c, p.5).

29. Schinasi et al (1990, esp. pp.144-149).

30. Akerlof (1990, Table 6, p.18).

31. Economic Bulletin (1991, p.2).

3 Changes in the Yugoslav financial and economic system

K. Ott

Yugoslavia

P34 P21

3.1 YUGOSLAV

Yugoslavia came into being in 1918 in areas which had before been ruled by, or under the dominant influence of, Austro-Hungary in the west and Turkey in the east. Until the Second World War Yugoslavia was a kingdom, whereafter it was transformed into a federal state. It now consists of six republics (Bosnia-Herzegovina, Croatia, Macedonia, Montenegro, Serbia and Slovenia) and two autonomous provinces (Kosovo and Vojvodina). Yugoslavia is made up of more or less mature nations and national minorities, with very different civilisational, cultural, historical and economic backgrounds. They speak different languages (Serbian, Croatian, Slovene and Macedonian), use different scripts (Latin and Cyrillic), and belong to various religions (Catholic, Orthodox, Islam).

Under the strong influence of the USSR and communist ideology, individuals and nations were completely suppressed, major emphasis being laid on the construction of socialism marked by a one-party system, centralisation of power, and negation of the market. All this caused great discontent, resulting in the last few years in a sharp polarisation, between two fundamental concepts: one a loose confederation or even dissolution, which is advocated by the republics of Croatia and Slovenia, and the other a unitary Yugoslavia, advocated by Serbia. Other republics vacillate between these two concepts. The western, more developed and richer republics, Slovenia and Croatia, advocate a faster introduction of a multiparty system and a market-oriented economy, while the less developed republics resist such changes. Discontent is steadily growing, differences are becoming greater, so that it is uncertain whether Yugoslavia will continue to exist even as a very loose confederation.

These introductory points are indispensable because, as will be seen below, they have decisively influenced changes in the financial system.

3.2 YUGOSLAV FINANCIAL SYSTEM

It is first necessary to describe the Yugoslav financial system, the institutions it consists of, and the reasons why the banking system must be discussed first. More specifically, even a first attempt to compare the Yugoslav financial system with western ones, necessarily produces the conclusion that the Yugoslav financial system and its institutions are markedly undeveloped and are still in a rudimentary stage.

Financial institutions in Yugoslavia can be classified in several ways. Under the earlier law, there were internal, basic and associated banks, and financial organisations (the post-office savings bank, savings bank and other savings and loan organisations, self-managing funds of associated labour, and other financial institutions). The new law provides for banks and other organisations (the post-office savings bank, savings bank, other savings and loan organisations, and other financial organisations). Although they formally exist, the significance of all financial organisations, with the exception of banks, is negligible. Banks in Yugoslavia hold 98 per cent of all the financial assets held by all financial institutions.

The central bank makes a distinction between monetary institutions whose liabilities include monetary obligations, that is, cash in circulation and clearing (giro) and other accounts through which they make payments (the federal, republican and provincial central banks, banks and the post-office savings bank) on the one hand, and other financial organisations which have no monetary obligations among their liabilities, on the other. Even from this perspective "other financial organisations" are not of any major significance.

Pension funds and insurance institutions were obliged to hold their resources in banks and were not allowed to invest them directly. Because of this, especially as a result of inflation, these resources have been devalued to such an extent that pension funds are now virtually worthless. Because of the non-existence of a financial market, the network of financial institutions linked to it is uncompleted.[1] Because of this structure of the financial system and the minor role played by all financial institutions – with the exception of banks – attention below will be mainly devoted to the Yugoslav banking system.

3.3 DEVELOPMENT AND PECULIARITIES OF THE YUGOSLAV BANKING SYSTEM

Yugoslav society has constantly been in the process of seeking its identity by trying out various systems and models. The development of the Yugoslav banking system frequently coincided with the phases of these changes, sometimes lagging behind and sometimes anticipating them. In fact, the Yugoslav banking system has gone through the following three main phases:

(1) *Period of State Management of the Economy (1945–51)*
Immediately after the Second World War, in the period from 1944 to 1946, the prewar market economy was, on the model of the Soviet Union, gradually replaced by a centrally-planned economic system. This was the beginning of state management in the economy in which the banking system was a constituent part of the centrally-run economy. The government managed the economy administratively; production and financial plans were laws. Credits and money simply supported the implementation of these plans, without having any active influence on economic development there were no commodity-monetary so relations in the market. The central bank performed, in addition through normal activities, the bulk of commercial bank operations: the so-called mono-bank system.

48

(2) *Period Beginning with the Introduction of Self-Management in Enterprises (1952–65)*

The introduction of workers' self-management began in 1952. Initially, workers' self-management did not exist in the entire economy, but only in enterprises. A dual situation was thus created in which at the macroeconomic level the state organised and directed the economy as a whole, while at the microeconomic level, in enterprises, there was workers' self-management. Banks continued to be state-run enterprises. They were founded by the state or narrower territorial administrative units, which also managed them.[2]

A complete monobank system was introduced – the central bank performed all banking operations: it issued money and gave short- and long-term credits. As early as 1954, communal and savings banks were being established, but the central bank continued directly to grant credit to their economy. At that time special credit institutions – social investment funds began also to be formed, and soon also specialised federal banks for foreign trade, investment and agriculture. Their obligations were guaranteed by the state. At the same time a social accountancy service was established, which subsequently developed into a powerful institution of the Yugoslav financial system, see below.

After 1961, the central bank became primarily the bankers' bank and no longer directly gave credit to the economy. There also emerged commercial banks of a general or specialised type. The central bank influenced banks' credit policy by means of credits, reserve requirements, and interest rates.

(3) *Period of the Extension of Self-Management to the Macroeconomic Level (1965–80)*

Although the periods 1945–52 and 1952–64 differed to some extent and the banking system was not quite the same, in both of them banks were exclusively founded by the state and narrower territorial administrative units. Things began substantially to change only as late as 1965. As a result of social and economic reforms self-management began to spread to the macroeconomic level as well, while the main role in founding and managing banks was taken over by enterprises.

This marked the beginning of the reduction of the state's role in the banking system: banks could now be founded by enterprises and banks, that is, not only by the state and narrower territorial administrative units. What is more, the latter could not have more than 20 per cent of votes at banks' meetings.

Banks became enterprises, which managed common resources on behalf of the community in line with general social interests and the framework set by the law. This change was to have enabled economic agents to manage their own monetary affairs, but in practice they did not succeed in realising this right. More specifically, the state ceased to shape the banks' credit policy, while enterprises, which were to have taken over this function, were unable to do this. Therefore this role was assumed by bank administrators. This gave rise to complaints about banks being "centres of alienated power"; something they should not be blamed for, because they simply had to find a way of coping with the newly-created situation.

In 1971, with the adoption of constitutional amendments, self-management was introduced at all levels of decision-making. At the same time the role of government authorities at the republican, provincial and local levels was strengthened. Existing enterprises were transformed into "basic organisations of associated labour" and "organisations of associated labour", and the whole economy was organised on the basis of self-management agreements and social compacts.

Investment and commercial banks were abolished and only banks and savings banks remained. Government authorities continued to participate in the founding of banks, but without voting rights and the right to profits. This period also saw a spontaneous process of organisation of financial departments, especially in large enterprises, which later on grew into, and were referred to as, internal banks. The process of freeing the banking system from state control was completed in 1977. From that year government authorities could no longer found banks, which, of course, did not mean that they did not influence bank operations. Internal banks were proclaimed to be the basic units of the banking system whose aim was to "unify labour and resources". The banking system was fragmented into countless small internal and commercial banks. These banks associated in associated banks, mainly at the republican or provincial level. All this led to the doubling or trebling of bank operations, bureaucratisation and the loss of links with economic realities.

(4) Period of a Gradual Transition to a Market Economy (1980s)
In essence, the Yugoslav banking system has gone through two periods, the turning point taking place in 1965. Until that year, all banks were state-run institutions. They could only be founded by the state and narrower territorial units, which, in addition to the central bank, exercised a strong influence on their operations. Enterprises did not have any influence on their founding, nor on their business, let alone households and individuals. There did not exist any workers' or social management in the banking sector. After 1965, the role of the state gradually began to weaken, and by 1977 it was completely eliminated. Banks could now be founded by enterprises, which shaped bank business policy at banks' meetings. However, the central bank continued to exercise a great influence on bank operations, and the influence of the state was not really diminished.

The early eighties saw an increasing deterioration in all segments of economic and social life; the causes of the crisis became evident and first attempts were made to change the situation. Various economic stabilisation programmes were adopted and there was increasing pressure towards a switch to a more market-oriented economy. Numerous new laws were passed, including a banking law.

3.4   ATTEMPTS AT CREATING AN ORIGINAL MODEL OF YUGOSLAV BANKING

Some attempts to make it distinctive have essentially determined the Yugoslav banking system, resulting in negative effects which will certainly be long lasting. The attempts to build up a new and different social, economic and political system, some quite specific organisational forms have been developed in Yugoslavia, along with commercial (basic) banks, more or less similar to those in other countries.

Internal Banks as the Basic Units of the Banking System

After 1965, the role of financial departments in enterprises were changed in a totally unorganised way and without any statutory grounds. There emerged a large number of variously organised financial departments,

51

especially in large enterprises, which began to be called internal banks. While internal banks greatly differed amongst themselves with respect to both organisation and functions, their main role was to monitor the use of resources of all the units of an enterprise, to deal with internal financial relations within enterprises, and to manage joint operations outside them. The status of internal banks was only subsequently regulated by a law, which defined them as the basic units of the country's entire banking and credit system. They had to be established by self-management agreements generated by basic and other organisations of associated labour (that is, enterprises). Their purpose was to ensure the realisation of social interests in monetary transactions and to monitor the movement of assets and income of each bank founder.

At that time it was considered that financial self-organisation of associated labour was a process which should lead to finding a new type of banking institution that would replace the previous ones which were then felt to be completely unacceptable in the Yugoslav system. The embryonic forms of this new type was the internal bank, which gradually grew into a complex and open monetary institution. The role of internal banks was primarily to pool monetary assets, to finance current operations and carry out development plans of the operating units of enterprises mutually linked in income-earning. Internal banks performed for the account of their members only those operations which the members could have performed for themselves: pooling resources and making payments. For this reason internal banks were not subjected to monetary regulation and some of them developed their financial activities to a considerable extent.

Internal and commercial banks had the same aims and tasks. However, the former were confined to concrete organisational forms and were not allowed to perform all banking operations, except through commercial banks. This primarily related to financial planning, pooling and procurement of resources, maintaining liquidity, and information-analytical operations. In seeking additional sources of credit for financing current business and development, enterprises still had to apply for the purpose to commercial banks, although through their internal banks. Enterprises had continuously to co-operate with both internal and commercial banks. Internal banks primarily acted here as intermediaries and representatives of their members' interests in commercial banks.

And yet, despite all their deficiencies, internal banks developed successfully and in 1988 their number exceeded 200. Regardless of their status, almost 50 per cent of the economy's financial resources was held in their accounts. Unfortunately, resources in the accounts of internal banks were less mobile than they would have been if kept in commercial banks, which operated in conformity with the normal principles of banking business. As can be seen, internal banks did not play any major role in granting credits to the economy. Enterprise borrowings from internal banks accounted for only a little more than 20 per cent of total borrowed funds. Internal banks mainly helped finance current business, and virtually played no major role in granting long-term credits. For long-term credits enterprises had to apply to commercial banks, a system which doubled administrative work.

Thus, in the long run, defining internal banks as the basic units of the banking system proved to be wrong. Instead of internal banks it would have been better to have enhanced development of commercial banks which should have assumed responsibility for their own business and that of the enterprises that had invested funds in them.

Associated Banks as Financiers of Megalomaniac Projects

As if it had not been enough to double administration in internal and basic (commercial) banks, another specific organisational form emerged in the Yugoslav banking system – *associated banks*. When the government assigned to banks the role of financing the economy, there emerged the problem of financing insatiable, gigantic and problematic projects (thermal power stations, the metal-working complex, the petrochemical industry, etc.). These projects were often economically unjustifiable and it was difficult to find anybody willing to finance them. A simple solution was found – banks were compelled to combine in associated banks, (mainly at the republican or provincial level). Huge amounts of resources were concentrated in these banks to finance large-scale projects.

The main function of associated banks was to pool resources of basic (commercial) banks, finance large-scale projects, perform foreign exchange operations and borrow funds on behalf of the basic banks – their members. In combining these functions, associated banks became very powerful. Enterprises now had to apply first to internal and then to commercial banks, and finally to associated banks. Thus administration was trebled, and the banking system became even more inefficient.

Each republic and province had one associated bank, whilst Serbia had two. Associated banks (for practical purposes) did not operate outside their territorial units. They were a powerful means for the latter as means to influence to not only banking business, but also economic and political life as a whole.

Management and Mode of Decision-Making

Here it is necessary to say a few words about management and decision-making. Banks in Yugoslavia are managed by their founders. They exercise this right at their meetings. A bank's executive body (executive committee) and its operative body (credit committee), are elected from amongst its founders. This means that members of a bank's credit and executive committee are not its employees but its founders, and this is where the main problem of bank management lies.

Social ownership is the main form of ownership in Yugoslavia (there is no state ownership, while private ownership is of minor significance). This means that those making decisions regarding the use of resources act on behalf of society and do not directly bear any consequences for the quality of their decisions. Thus, since decisions are made by bank founders, and not by bank employees and experts, the former can allocate funds to themselves without paying too much attention to their own credit standing. As a result, the biggest debtors virtually control their banks, pushing them into ever-bigger debts and losses. Banks are not able to refuse credits to big debtors precisely because they are those who make key decisions.

A refusal to assign funds to a big enterprise could bring on to the streets a mass of dissatisfied workers. To calm them down, they are promised higher salaries, and to pay these banks approve the necessary funds. To enable banks to provide such funds, the government prints increasing amounts of money. This starts an unbroken chain leading the country into an ever deeper crisis.

It is important to emphasise that, at least until recently, enterprises were rarely liquidated due to losses. In Yugoslavia there is a very low mobility of manpower, social protection of unemployed workers is inadequate, and workers see in their enterprises the only guarantee of survival. Because of this, peaceful behaviour by dissatisfied workers was for a long time bought by concessions – tolerance of surplus labour and idleness, low but guaranteed salaries, non-dismissal, etc. Precisely because of the above problems, the government strives to control banks and to exercise through them political and economic influence. This brings us to a very important issue – that of personnel policy. The same people were rotated from enterprises to banks, from banks to government and party bodies. This made it impossible to make profit-oriented economic decisions, since all decisions were aimed at sustaining the prevailing socio-political system, while the economic system was pushed into the background.

It has recently become clear to everybody that changes are indispensable. Profit-oriented banks should be managed by experts not connected with political bodies. Concrete decisions regarding use and channelling of resources should not be made by bank founders themselves.

General Assessment of Banks

The above-described development of the Yugoslav banking system, its role as a servant of the government and economy, its specific forms and the modes of business developed in it, have brought this system into its present situation from which it is difficult to find a way out. Banks, like all other segments of society, were neither market nor independent institutions. In their business operations they were not guided by the wish to make profit and increase their capital. In granting credits they were not primarily guided by the assessment of the profitability of such credits.

The setting in which the banks operated – social ownership and strong political influences – meant that no attention was paid to profitability. Risks were dispersed and losses were covered by all – the government, successful enterprises, and even private individuals (through inflation). Accustomed to operating through directives received from political circles, banks have suddenly found themselves in a vacuum. The government no longer wishes, nor is it able, to cover losses, the number of successful firms is ever smaller, households are getting poorer and poorer, and savings are shrinking (especially in domestic banks). Everybody is talking about market principles, competition, profit and assessment of credit standing. Banks with their own accumulated losses and the losses of their clients, with oversised staff inert and inefficient, are not able to immediately adopt principles respected in market economies.

3.5   THE CENTRAL BANK

The various phases of the country's development has influenced changes in both commercial banking and the central bank system. The central bank was nationalised in 1946 and dove-tailed into the process of concentration of banking and preparations for the transition to a planned economy. In addition to its money-issue function, the central bank became the principal institution for giving short-term credits and for money transfers at home and abroad, implementation of the budgets, and operating savings deposits.[3] Out of a total of 582 banks in the country, 437 belonged to the central bank. With the introduction of a monobank system in 1952, all banks in the country were merged with the central bank, which now issued money and gave short- and long-term credits. In this way an attempt was made to ensure appropriate government record-keeping and control of banking business, and to provide support for the development of the economic system.

Two years later although the monobank system was abandoned, the central bank remained not only the bankers' bank and bank of issue, but also the organiser of money transfers, supervision, record-keeping and statistics. It gave credits not only to banks, but also to large enterprises and the government. Interest rates were artificially kept low so that they had no influence on investment and saving, and so no role in the efficient channelling of funds.

Only in the early sixties did the central bank begin to act primarily as the bankers' bank and issue bank. Granting credit to the economy was transferred to banks, and internal money transfers to the Social Accountancy Service. The central bank was a unitary organisation responsible to the federal assembly and federal government. With the granting of greater powers to the republics and provinces at the beginning of the seventies a system of central banks (federal, republican and provincial) was introduced. The objectives of monetary and credit policy were determined by the federal assembly, and the system of central banks was responsible for its implementation, for currency stability, general payment liquidity and the implementation of jointly determined foreign exchange policy. The board of governors consists of the governor of the federal central bank and the governors of the republican and provincial central banks. At that time most decisions of the board of governors were made unanimously. The governor of the federal central bank is appointed by the federal assembly.

The central bank most frequently restrained credits, interest rates were rigid and low and there were not open-market operations (nor was there any financial market!). Deposits kept by banks in the central bank were from time to time frozen. The measures taken were more or less ineffective, and as in the mid-seventies the rate of inflation began to rise. In the eighties, the central bank assumed a significant role in rescheduling external debts. Increasing influence was now exercised by the International Monetary Fund, which insisted on an increase in interest rates. This was not in accord with the economic policy pursued so the central bank was increasingly in a conflict between past experience and new demands.

Under the pressure of foreign creditors, the central bank assumed control over the country's external debt and issued guarantees for new borrowing. Decisions of the board of governors were no longer made unanimously, but by a majority vote. This weakened the position of the republics and provinces whose protests kept growing. The International Monetary Fund, like the World Bank, made new credits conditional on a reduction of the budget deficit, abolition of price controls, a rise in interest rates in accordance with inflation, and devaluation of the dinar. As a result, the central bank and the country as a whole were confronted with numerous new problems and compelled to start making changes.

Reasons for the Inefficiency of the Central Bank

Regardless of occasional variations in the movement of savings, investment and the amount of money in circulation, it can be concluded that, in the long run, the main problem of the central bank was constant and enormous pressure for the creation of additional money. The reason primarily lay in an acute shortage of capital, the wish to accelerate capital formation, and relatively low domestic saving. Low productivity was always explained by this capital shortage, so that efforts were made to speed capital formation as much as possible. Neither government nor private saving in Yugoslavia can be compared with the rate of saving in developed countries, either *per capita* or in overall terms. The low level of domestic saving could be explained in part by the country's general poverty, insufficient tradition and non-existence of adequate financial institutions which would stimulate various forms of saving. However, much responsibility lay with enormous government expenditure. Even in the periods when *per capita* income grew, most of this growth was almost always spent. Exaggerated subsidies to inefficient enterprises and entire economic branches and regions only augmented this expenditure.

As a result of relatively scarce saving and a great appetite for investment, along with covering the losses of inefficient enterprises and branches, credit expansion was stimulated both with the central bank and the banking sector as a whole. The government required the central bank to create money in order to achieve what is financed elsewhere by taxes. The central bank gradually took over government debt, thus increasing the volume of money in circulation. In implementing monetary policy it relied on reserve requirements, interest rates and credit restraints. These instruments might have perhaps by themselves been sufficient for the implementation of monetary policy had there not been an unsatiated hunger for credits. The problem was that the central bank was often unable to harmonise the objectives of monetary policy with low interest rates. When the central bank faced inflationary pressure it was not able effectively both to restrict credit and maintain low interest rates. In short, the central bank was required to maintain low interest rates, frequently lower than those in capital-rich countries, to ensure successful government financing, regardless of the magnitude of its debt and the failure of fiscal policy, and to lend to unsuccessful enterprises and entire branches and regions, regardless of their continued inefficiency.

It is therefore understandable that in the course of the seventies and eighties, financing the government's fiscal deficit was the main cause of initially moderate and subsequently inevitably ever-higher inflation, and finally hyperinflation. It is often maintained that, except for loans to the army, the central bank was not a direct creditor of the government. And yet, taking over the rate-of-exchange differences of commercial banks, giving selective credits to individual activities or regions, and similar parafiscal transactions are in essence tantamount to financing government deficits.[4] It need not be especially emphasised that this state of affairs contributed to increasing money creation, a rise in inflation and the overall impoverishment of the country.

3.6 CHANGES IN THE LAST FEW YEARS

As already stated, commercial banks were executors of orders given by large enterprises, which were at the same time the biggest debtors, so that the banks were not able to operate in accordance with basic banking principles, nor to channel funds into projects that would yield the highest or fastest returns. The central bank was fully integrated into this banking system. It supported and managed it. Instead of confining itself to making monetary policy, the central bank also shaped credit policy and maintained direct relations with the economy and government. As a result, both monetary and credit policies were inadequate. The consequences were failed investments, indebtedness at home and abroad, inflation, grey money issue, etc.

Changes in Commercial Banking

Frustrated banks, a discontented economy and an insatiable state compelled the federal government at the beginning of 1988 to initiate a reform of the economic system.[5] Bitter discussions lasted one year. A greater role of the market was advocated along with the diversification of saving, introduction of securities, establishment of new types of financial institutions, access to private capital, and many other nice things. However, the final version of the reform document was not very radical. In February 1989, the federal assembly passed an inconsistent and deficient law, which has, ever since its passage been constantly amended and supplemented. In short, the new law created:

a) a new type of independent self-managed bank which, in addition to ensuring liquidity and asset security, should operate to make profits. Every bank can now independently fix interest rates and charges for its services. Distinctions between basic, associated and internal banks have been abolished. The law provides for universal commercial banks and for the possibility of founding specialised banking institutions. It also allows foreign investment in the banking system and the formation of joint-stock banks wholly or partly owned by foreigners.

b) Only social legal entities may be original bank founders, while other domestic and foreign natural and legal persons may only become subsequent bank founders with lesser rights. At least ten founders are required to establish a bank and they must invest a specific amount of dinars in its capital stock, for which they obtain appropriate securities.

c) A bank's reserves are formed from part of the profit the bank makes through its business, and they also serve to cover risks. The level of risk will depend on the amount of resources in the bank's capital stock and reserves.

d) Individual credits may amount to maximum 20 per cent of the bank's capital stock.

e) Members of a bank's executive board are elected from among its founders, but also a specific number of its employees may sit on it. Decisions regarding the formation, composition and competence of the credit committee are left to the bank's meetings.

f) Provisions concerning a bank's liquidity, solvency and bankruptcy have been markedly stiffened.

As soon as it was passed, the new law was subject to sharp criticism. It has since been amended, largely with a view to making it possible to establish banks as joint-stock companies or limited liability companies, found by mixed banks, equalise the rights of domestic and foreign founders, raise the limits of credit that may be given to individual credit-seekers, etc. However, some problems have not been adequately solved even by these amendments. The rights of private and social investors in banks have not been fully equalised, founders still exercise too great an influence on concrete decisions concerning banks' business, bank directors do not have sufficient powers, there is not enough room for the diversification of the banking system and strengthening the role of other financial institutions, the question of banks' supervision and the role of the central bank in it has not been adequately solved, etc.

Needless to say, in order to improve the banking system it is not sufficient even though necessary to change the law. It is also necessary to create some other preconditions, primarily to ensure the democratisation of society, political freedoms, possibilities for independent economic decision-making, less regulation, respect for individuals' interests, independence and equality of all in all parts of the country.

Changes in the Central Bank System

It was neccessary to amend the provisions of the federal and republican constitutions relating to the central bank, and to enact a new central bank law. Because of the unsuccessful performance of the central bank's basic duties, deteriorating conditions in the country, the economic and social reform, attempts at establishing a market-oriented economy, and the reassessment of relations within the federation. Despite numerous disagreements among the republics, in these amendments the view favouring greater centralisation prevailed. They provide for more homogeneity and a stronger role of the central bank in monetary policy-making, restrict the powers of the central banks of the republics and provinces, strive to introduce more order in government spending, change the role of the board of governors and the governor of the federal central bank himself; political control over the work of the central bank is no longer exercised by the federal government, but by the federal assembly.

Considered from this aspect, these changes sound fairly logical. However, the new, and seeming, autonomy of the central bank has not proved effective enough. There are still difficulties in resolving problems emerging in the work of the board of governors, in relations among the federal, republican and provincial central banks, in relations between the central bank and the federal assembly. The federal government seems at first glance to have been left out of the game. Problems prevailing in a very disunited country cannot be solved by insistence on homogeneity. Unitarily-conceived and implemented measures tend more frequently to have different rather than similar consequences for individual regions or

61

activities. The impact of similar measures, for example of credit policy, cannot under conditions of unequal living standards have the same consequences in various parts of the country. In situations where measures must be quickly taken usually contradictory interests lead to non-economically motivated concessions. This only further complicates a situation which is already difficult to solve.

3.7 PROGRAMME OF THE FEDERAL GOVERNMENT

The late eighties saw a further aggravation of the crisis and a further deterioration of the economic situation, marked by disequilibrium in the economy, indebtedness, great losses incurred by enterprises and banks, structural disproportions, technological backwardness and an inflation tending to attain an annual rate of 1,000 per cent. The federal government realised that it was necessary to build up an economic and political system which would ensure economic efficiency and political democracy. It adopted a programme which should in the course of five years pull the country out of the crisis, revive the economy and ensure dynamic development. By many changes in relevant laws it tried first to provide basic preconditions for an integral market, pluralism of ownership, identification of title holders of social ownership, and the country's inclusion in the world market.

The concept of economic policy laid down in the programme is based on three pillars: convertibility of the dinar, a deflation strategy and fiscal and monetary policy. The dinar was devalued and pegged to the DM. Convertibility related to all current transactions at home and abroad, and every citizen had the right to exchange unlimited amounts of dinars for foreign currency in banks.[6] The government considered that there was a rationale for convertibility. It saw them in a favourable balance-of-payments situation, that is, a rise in foreign exchange reserves of £2.9 billion, which is two and a half times more than is normally required to meet external obligations.[7]

Needless to say, the government envisaged measures also relating to the financial sector. For the first time the budget has, in addition to its fiscal function, an active role in economic policy. Thus, the federal budget has fully taken over obligations stemming from part of foreign credits (about 70 per cent of these credits go to economically undeveloped parts of the country). Furthermore, it has taken over a considerable part of dubious bank assets, so-called contaminated credits. A special agency for the financial rehabilitation of banks will be set up by the central bank, and until its formation rehabilitation affairs will be conducted by the central bank on behalf and for the account of the federation. The budget also allocates £123 million for the purpose. The territorial units should act in a similar way.

The central bank is relieved of affairs which do not actually fall within its sphere of business and are a cause of uncontrolled money creation and inflation. Part of the obligations of the central bank has been transferred to the budget and transformed into public debt. Clearing account balances should no longer be monetised, the central bank should not lend to the federations and selective crediting should be abandoned.

Bank must strive to make profits and are compulsorily transformed into joint-stock companies. Both domestic persons and foreigners may be shareholders.

In short, the programme is based on the convertibility of the dinar in current transactions with other countries, and the right of private persons freely to exchange dinars for foreign exchange at the then official rate of 7 dinars to the German mark. To this should be added a firm monetary policy, balancing the budget by its own real revenues, free formation of interest rates and prices, limitation of wages, and solution of the problems of banks, enterprises and social programmes through the budget.

Critique of the Government's Programme

From its very inception the government's programme was subjected to numerous critiques, many of which have proved to be correct. The programme tried to achieve contradictory aims – to put an end to hyperinflation and create an open economy adjusted to the world market. Owing to low productivity, a combination of deregulation of imports, reduced tariff protection and an overvalued dinar, have almost ruined the economy.

Inflation was arrested after only four months and already by that time the level of internal prices had exceeded the dinar's rate of exchange by over 70 per cent. The over-valued dinar hindered exports, the growth of foreign exchange reserves first slowed down. Thereafter they began to decrease and citisens rushed to the banks. Financial indiscipline and the unauthorised use of high-powered money followed, and at the beginning of 1991 monthly inflation was 6 – 7 per cent.

It could be said that the programme was fairly successful in the first half of 1990 (fixed exchange rates and restrictive monetary policy), however, because of the non-fulfilment of all its parts the programme was found to fail. More specifically, measures envisaged to strengthen financial discipline, the restructuring of banks and enterprises failed, the fiscal system was not adequately changed and most important of all the government continued to spend too much at all levels.

Implementation of the Federal Government's Programme and Latest Developments in the Financial Sector

Attempts to Transform Social Capital
With the introduction of workers' self-management in Yugoslavia state ownership was abolished and social ownership in the economy introduced. At the time this was considered to be a great step forward in the construction of a new and more equitable society. This development now hinders the process of the economy's transformation because it is difficult to determine the actual owners of social capital, the prevalent form of ownership in the economy.

Re-nationalisation is considered to be a step backward, because we had already experienced it, and it is well-known that a state-run economy is in principle less efficient than private. To find a proper mode of privatisation seems to be an almost impossible task.

The federal government has offered one of the possible ways of transforming social ownership. The model has met with numerous critiques and in some republics has been rejected in full. As a result, the transformation of social ownership is proceeding slowly and in varied ways.

According to the relevant federal law – which is not applied in all republics – socially-owned enterprises may on the basis of social capital obtain additional funds by issuing shares, or through the sale of enterprise shares.[8]

In order to avoid nationalisation of social property, enterprises may also issue shares at a discount. These are internal shares which can not be traded on a stock exchange. Internal shares can be sold to present and former enterprise workers, to other individuals, and to pension funds. The law provides for various percentages for sales and discounts. Owners of internal shares acquire the right to participate in profits and in enterprise management.

The proposed mode of ownership transformation substantially differs from changing owners in market economies. In contrast to open and public sale of enterprises on the capital market, internal shares will be issued in Yugosalvia. They will only become external shares in the next phase and will only then be quoted on the market.

The proposed programme of transformation is either proceeding very slowly, or not at all. The reasons for this are numerous and they are compounded by ideological obstacles, lack of domestic capital in the country, and by an unfavourable political and economic situation which does not stimulate investment of foreign capital. An especially significant problem is the determination of prices of securities, that is, by issuing enterprises. The market is not developed and prices cannot be formed on it. In addition, security issuers do not wish to offer their shares on the market lest their prices should rapidly fall. The shares are overvalued owing to the accounting system which keeps a record of the book value of assets, a value which has nothing to do with the real one. A special problem is the possible transformation of internal into external shares, which the law does not define at all.

The solution of the ownership issue is also crucial for banks. More specifically, bank's founders are enterprises and as long as they have not solved the question of their owners banks' transformation is not possible. Defining ownership is itself not sufficient, but it is necessary also to solve the problem of the relationship between the owners and the management of enterprises especially banks. This is a long-term process and options are numerous.

3.8   INTRODUCTION OF SECURITIES

Securities and stock exchanges have virtually not existed in postwar Yugoslavia, with the exception of negligible issue of state securities. The package of new laws passed in 1989 and 1990 also provides for the establishment of money and capital markets and issue of securities.

Securities are understood to include shares, bonds, treasury notes, certificates of deposit and commercial bills. They may be issued by enterprises, banks and other financial organisations, insurance institutions and any other legal persons.

This was met by great euphoria among the public at large, securities were intensively published and presented as a magic formula for the solution of all financial and investment problems.

According to foreign models, a federal securities and exchange commission has been set up. It gives permits for the issue of long-term securities and the start-up of stock exchanges, and proposes measures for the prevention of harmful effects of speculative transactions on stock exchanges.

No permit of the securities and exchange commission is required from issuers of shares if founding joint-stock companies (that is, at first issue), nor from socio-political communities issuing securities. In this respect the Yugoslav law-maker has taken account of the solutions in other countries in which the government is the most reliable issuer, while in Yugoslavia it is the most unreliable one. In addition, no approval by the commission is necessary for the issue of internal shares since they are not intended for the market.

In the course of 1990, 51 long-term securities issues were approved in Yugoslavia to a total value of £156 million, mainly in the form of shares. Shares were mainly issued by banks for the purpose of increasing capital stock, but also of meeting the requirements imposed by the law. Bonds were mainly issued by enterprises with a view to obtaining funds for investment activities, modernisation of technology and financing current production. In short, the number of issues (51) and the number of securities quoted on the stock exchanges was small (14 in Ljubljana and one in Belgrade).

The reasons for the low interest in issuing long-term securities are numerous, the main ones being almost certainly the unfavourable political and economic situation, lack of capital, and the unsolved question of social ownership.

Because of the undeveloped primary market the volume of transactions on the stock exchanges is relatively modest (although one could look at it the other way round!). This modest volume of business is also partly due to the reluctance of issuers to be confronted with the possibility of the prices of their securities being lowered by the market. This especially relates to banks which have only formally been established as joint-stock companies. Furthermore, the problem of the revaluation of capital stock has not yet been regulated. There is reluctance to convert internal shares into external ones, since owing to the obsolete accounting system it is difficult to have confidence in the estimates of issuers' credit standing. The government does not issue securities. Experts in the financial departments of enterprises are not sufficiently conversant with possibilities offered by securities (or are perhaps too conversant with their employees circumstances!).

In order to stimulate the issue of and trade in securities financial experts suggest various solutions, such as the involvement of a larger number of brokers and participants (including private individuals) in stock exchange transactions, introduction of tax breaks, issue of government securities and their quotation on stock exchanges, and generally, ensuring economic and not only regulatory conditions for the issue of and trade in securities.

Needless to say, such economic conditions are difficult to create, but changes in the relevant legislation are already under way in this direction.

Stock Exchange Transactions

At the beginning of 1990, political leaders in Belgrade and Ljubljana competed to be the first to open a stock exchange. According to the law, stock exchanges could be founded by banks and other financial organisations (which, as already stated, virtually did not exist). Social funds, enterprises and other legal entities could through the intermediary of authorised participants also be founders, but all this largely reduced itself to compelling banks to be founders. The race was won by Belgrade, but the stock exchange in Ljubljana proved to be incomparably more successful (due to the great interest and involvement of the leading and almost the only significant bank in Slovenia).

The Ljubljana stock exchange began to operate in March 1990. It met twice a week, with 62 meetings held until the end of the year. By then it had recorded a turnover of £4,800,000. Sixteen securities issues (13 bonds, one share and two treasury notes) were quoted, and almost 87 per cent of the overall turnover was accounted for by clearing account claims.

The Belgrade stock exchange began to operate in February last year and has since held 43 meetings, but the volume of business has been negligible. At its meetings bonds of the Republic of Serbia – the Republican Fund for Undeveloped Regions – were traded, and almost the entire turnover of £2,685 was realised at only one meeting. In addition to these bonds at the Belgrade stock exchange only shares of one bank (from Croatia!) are quoted.[9]

A stock exchange was opened in Zagreb in April 1989 but it has not yet begun to operate.

3.9   FINANCIAL REHABILITATION OF COMMERCIAL BANKS

The causes of losses incurred by commercial banks have largely been defined – the biggest bank owners were at the same time the principal users of bank credits; there was too large a concentration of credits on a small number of credit users, relevant legislation did not offer the possibility of insurance against losses, business supervision was inadequate, the influence of the central bank was insufficient, and the accounting system obsolete.

Bank losses are differently estimated: according to some they amount to £4.5 billion, according to others to £7 billion, and according to yet others to £10 billion pounds. Bank representatives themselves maintain that these sums are exaggerated and that some of the credits given are not yet lost. According to one of the more recent estimates, losses amount to close on 40 per cent of banks' assets, or close on 60 per cent of deposits. This is three times more than the banks' capital stock.[10]

The federal government proposes general or linear financial rehabilitation of banks through the central bank and the Federal Agency for Securing Deposits and Financial Rehabilitation of Banks. The Agency would temporarily (for six months) purchase banks' bad losses to improve their position and arrest a further rise in losses. The Agency would issue bonds for the amount of losses taken over. It would be also able to purchase potential losses with credits obtained from the central bank. Commercial banks would have to buy securities of the central bank for the amount of these credits. The Agency would conclude an agreement with each bank regarding the conditions it should satisfy during the time it uses these funds earmarked for financial support.

There is also a proposal for the formation of a federal Treasury. The federation would be separate from the central bank and would be able itself to manage budgetary resources and invest them as short-term funds on financial markets.[11] The idea of a federal Treasury has been met with great resistance. Such a Treasury is not in accordance with the federal constitution, but in Yugoslavia such things are nothing new. In addition, in this way the federation would directly, without the intermediation of the central bank, maintain contacts with banks and the central bank would not be able independently to influence monetary policy.

There are many problems regarding the financial rehabilitation of banks and nothing has yet been done to cope with them. £500 million has been earmarked from high-powered money, but this is not enough because from £750 million to £1 billion are need annually. Another problem is that the republics do not wish any financial rehabilitation at the federal level, because they trust neither the federal government nor the central bank. Furthermore, no agreement has been reached on criteria for allocating government securities to individual banks (for example, whether according to the volume of private dinar or foreign exchange deposits guaranteed by the central bank, that is, the federation).

At present, federal bodies insist on a concept according to which a general financial rehabilitation should be carried out at the federal level. If such a rehabilitation fails, individual financial rehabilitation procedures will be resorted to – on a case to case basis – at the republican level. Since neither the federation nor individual republics have money for such rehabilitation, it is expected that the dilemma will be solved so that the republics which have funds will alone financially rehabilitate their banks. Some republics have already announced this, and perhaps they will succeed in procuring the necessary funds.

In any case, financial rehabilitation of banks should also be linked to changes in the ownership relation with enterprises whose founders are still the banks' biggest debtors.

3.10   INSTANCES OF FINANCIAL INDISCIPLINE

Financial indiscipline prevails in all forms in the country as a whole. However, what happened at the end of 1990 is unprecedented, even in Yugoslavia's history rich in financial scandals.

Ever since the time of the state-run planned economy, the central bank has traditionally been considered as a refuge for all those who could not otherwise come by funds. Thus, for example, even the present relatively stiff federal regulations regarding the maximal daily use of banks' reserve requirements of up to 10 per cent are not generally respected. Some banks have used up to as much as 90 per cent of the reserves. Credits for liquidity (with a prescribed maximum of 100 per cent of investment in treasury bills subscribed with the central bank) are regularly exceeded. One bank used such credits to an amount exceeding 35 times the allowed sum! The central bank should exclude from the market banks which infringe discipline in this way, but information thereon comes late and the central bank does not have a timely insight into banks' financial situation.

The peak of monetary indiscipline (about which the federal government was informed by an anonymous letter) was reached at the end of 1990. After all sources of funds from taxes and tariffs, reserve requirements and credits for liquidity were exhausted, the assembly of the republic of Serbia simply passed at the proposal of the republican government a law providing for the use of credits from high-powered money.[12]

In this way, through its national bank and without the knowledge of the board of governors of the central bank, Serbia made use of high-powered money in excess of the limit set by a joint decision on monetary and credit policy. This so-called "giral" (credit) money was issued and placed in the account of Serbia and the accounts of some Serbian banks.

These credits from high-powered money amounted to £680 million, or to about half the total amount of planned credits from high-powered money in 1991 for Yugoslavia as a whole. Of this total, £186 million was allocated for pensions, £300 million for liquidity, and £194 million for agriculture.

This caused a great scandal and stirred still further inter-republican and inter-nationality disputes. Part of the money was prevented from being used, and part – especially that for pensions – was irretrievably lost. The federal government tried to exploit this case for strong centralisation, and its adversaries for still stronger attacks on the government's programme.

Attempts are now being made to solve the problem by a compromise.

Serbia, its republican national bank and commercial banks should return the funds taken from high-powered money. Needless to say, they are no longer able to do so.

The central bank has until further notice stopped any use of credits from high-powered money. This also applies to those central and commercial banks which have not done anything wrong. At the suggestion of the federal government, changes in legislation are being sought to abolish the accounts of the republican central banks. There would be only a single account of the federal central bank for the use of high-powered money and a single account for the performance of money transfers. In addition, it is intended to empower the governor of the central bank to remove from office governors of the republican central banks (this right is now vested in the republican assemblies).

The republics resist changes that would strengthen the federal government because they do not offer any guarantee and protection from new abuses. In large parts of the country all sources of funds (depreciation, etc.) and fiscal sources have been spent, so that a similar way of "financing" could also easily occur at the federal level.

The republics are now faced with the dilemma of whether they should themselves act in a similar way and to create money without authorisation and thus contribute to inflation, whose consequences will be borne by all others, or somehow to protect themselves from the consequences of the use of false money. Various methods are used. Some republics try to emulate Serbia's example, but federal authorities are cautious and react more quickly. In any case, it can be expected that inflation will again be high this year.

Because of all this, it is now deliberated whether or not to introduce republican currencies. The federal constitution and federal laws provide for a single monetary system, but a tendency towards greater monetary decentralisation is evident. Strong pressure is especially being exerted in the more developed republics (Croatia, Slovenia), in which the view prevails that financial stability is the basic precondition for the reform. Various options are being considered, from linking the domestic currency to a foreign one to the introduction of parallel currencies.

It is obvious that reluctance to finance increasing government needs, bearing the costs of inflation caused by other federal units, and the need for a stable currency in parts of the country which want to develop their own economies, will intensify the growing striving for emancipation in the monetary sphere too. However, monetary sovereignty is only a part of the country's overall sovereignty and it does not depend on the decisions of financial experts but rather on those of politicians.

3.11 CONCLUSION

Political insecurity, lack of confidence in the government and fear of an uncertain future can also be seen from data on banks' operations. In 1990, the central bank sold on the domestic foreign exchange market foreign exchange to an amount of £2 billion and bought £590 million. Banks sold to households £2.8 billion and purchased from them £1.5 billion, a net outflow of £1.3 billion. Less than 1 per cent of this amount was used for the purchase of goods and services, 52 per cent was placed in private foreign exchange accounts, and 47 per cent was paid in cash.

These data are indicative of households' mistrust of banks and the government. Households were for years encouraged to buy foreign exchange and keep it in domestic banks. The federal government's programme allowed the possibility of buying foreign exchange in banks. Households made use of this possibility and invested large amounts in banks. Now, for several months it has not been possible to withdraw foreign exchange from bank accounts. Some banks offer the possibility of withdrawing foreign exchange deposits in dinars, and some do not offer even this possibility. Since the dinar's rate of exchange is over-valued (officially one DM is worth 9 and unofficially 13 dinars), the households have been badly hurt.

The federal government perhaps rightly realised what should be done to revive the economy. It seems, however, that the timing was wrong. The government's programme provided for greater federal powers, and greater centralisation, while the processes of democratisation (both globally and locally) marked by free elections, a multiparty system, revival of nationalism also created tendencies towards decentralisation and emancipation. Because of all this, political clashes and pressures have gradually completely paralysed the work of the federation, the federal government and federal bodies and agencies. The envisaged objectives of the reform have not been attained, the federal government has been endangered, and so has the survival of the state as a whole.

However, regardless of the significance of the political situation and its impact on the realisation or non-realisation of the reform programme, economic aspects have played an even more decisive role. Provided it survives in its present form, and each of its republics separately, Yugoslavia will be confronted with the same problems in the case of its disintegration.

It is very difficult to make it possible for an inefficient and unproductive economy to open up to and join the world market. Therefore, until its structure has been changed a certain form of protection, either through tariffs or via a favourite rate of exchange, is indispensable. New investment is not possible without increasing production and arresting the fall in employment.

The objective of the reform should be to revive the economy, raise productivity and employment and increase investments, stabilise the domestic currency and ensure all those fine parameters which economists like to emphasise. For the time being, the situation in Yugoslavia is anything but that, production is declining, employment is falling, investment is decreasing, and so is the value of the dinar. For any kind of improvement in these trends it is necessary to determine some priorities, which certainly include bringing order in the financial system.

To bring the financial system in order it is certainly necessary to define the position and role of the central bank. It is indispensable to separate the central bank from parafiscal functions, put a stop to the use of high-powered money whenever somebody finds it necessary, ensure its independence, and enable it to take care of and ensure the stability of the national currency. It is also indispensable financially to rehabilitate banks and enterprises.

The fulfilment or non-fulfilment of the federal government's programme can serve as a good lesson. The government succeeded in establishing a fixed rate of exchange and for quite a long time to pursue a firm and restrictive monetary policy, but it failed to ensure financial discipline and to carry out ownership transformation in banks and enterprises. In addition, what is perhaps most important, the government has not succeeded in restricting its expenditure.

If there is a return of hyperinflation, and everything points out to it,

73

Yugoslavia will again find itself where it was, but economic indicators will be worse than ever before.

The failed attempt at an economic reform is perhaps only an indicator of the impossibility of a successfully political reform in Yugoslavia. This is perhaps one of the last chances of discussing Yugoslavia's financial system, because maybe there will soon be no Yugoslavia any more.

POST SCRIPTUM
22 August 1991

The forecast I made in the last sentence of my chapter written only four months ago is already coming true. Two of the six republics have in the meantime proclaimed their independence. This has been followed by intervention by the federal army and many dead and wounded. One of the republics—Slovenia—is, thanks to its homogeneity, on the way to emancipation, and the other—Croatia—has been drawn into civil war.

Developments in the banking and economic system cannot but follow those in the political sphere. The federal government—considered by many to be the last cohesive factor in the country—has discredited itself by taking part in military intervention. Its programme for overcoming the crisis has no longer any chance today.

The country is in deep recession, the balance of payment rapidly deteriorating, foreign exchange reserves are dwindling, and inflation is accelerating. The official exchange rate of the pound is 38 dinars, as compared with 60 unofficially.

After the proclamation of independence to the two republics, the Board of Governors of the National Bank of Yugoslavia excluded them from the monetary system. These republics may not obtain any credits from base money, nor any cash, nor may they operate on the foreign exchange market, while the National Bank of Yugoslavia refuses to give consent to credit arrangements concluded by their banks with foreign partners. This is in fact of no importance, because under the present conditions no foreign credits are anyhow available; the foreign exchange market has this year operated only 25 days and all those who wish to do so take credits from high-powered money.

Citizens in vain besiege bank windows to withdraw their foreign exchange savings, and many banks are not even able to pay the dinar counter value for foreign exchange savings.

In a country in which airports are closed and roads blocked by barriers, problems such as the transformation of social capital, financial rehabilitation of banks, introduction of securities and securities markets are, despite all efforts exerted by experts, of peripheral importance.

NOTES

1. The unusual role played by the financial sector in Yugoslavia is also shown by the way it is treated in the classification of activities. In line with the Marxist classification, financial services are categorised among non-production economic activities and grouped under so-called "Financial and Other Services", which consists of banking, life and property insurance, transport services, project design and related services, geological prospecting, research and development, and business services(!). Nor is the number of staff working in these activities impressive. Those employed in the banking sector account for 1.21 per cent of the total labour force in the country.
2. Administrative units in Yugoslavia are: the Federation, Republics, Provinces and Communes.
3. At the time of food etc. rationing it even issued cheques and ration cards to households.
4. According to a report of the World Bank, accumulated losses in the Yugoslav central bank 7.1 billion amounted to somewhat more than 60 per cent of its overall assets, or about 24 per cent of the gross national product in 1987. Over 70 per cent was accounted for by covering losses incurred through rate-of-exchange differences, the rest by foreign borrowings of the central bank and the taking over of losses of specific groups of enterprises, mainly in the undeveloped parts of the country.
5. At that time there were in Yugoslavia 150 basic, 9 associated and more than 200 internal banks.
6. The Yugoslav currency was last time convertible in 1931. The 1931 convertibility was wrongly timed, that is, precisely at the moment when other countries were abandoning it – and lasted only a hundred days.
7. All amounts in the text have been computed at an exchange rate of 26.81 dinars to the pound.
8. Social capital is an enterprise's equity capital diminished by a proportionate part of uncovered losses, and a proportionate part of reserves and other funds.
9. Banks did not show any interest whatsoever in the Belgrade stock exchange. Not a single bank appeared at 32 out of a total of 43 meetings, representatives

of one bank attended nine meetings, and only two meetings were attended by representatives of more than one bank. Not a single member has sent his comments on the annual report and on the proposed measures for expanding business dispatched to all members of the stock exchange.

10. At the beginning of 1989, there were 200 internal, 145 basic and 9 associated banks in Yugoslavia. After changes made in accordance with the law, there are today altogether 78 commercial banks with a business potential of 20,283 million pounds. Croatia has relatively the largest number of banks and its system is the most dispersed, while Serbia has the largest share in bank business potential. Twenty-one per cent of banks account for 80 per cent and one bank accounts for over 20 per cent of aggregate bank business potential.

11. Needless to say, because of the republics' reluctance to finance the federation (they do not even pay taxes and tariffs into the federal budget) the federal governments' principal problem is to procure some funds.

12. In Yugoslavia the amount of credits from high-powered money for the country as a whole is determined by the board of governors of the central bank.

4 Development of capital and financial markets in Hungary

K.J. Corner

4.1 HISTORY

During the eighteenth and nineteenth century the banking system in Hungary developed in a similar way to many other continental countries. This resulted in the predominance of universal banks. There were also a large number of small banks with extensive branch networks. A sizeable proportion of these banks were at town and county levels, but these were controlled by a small number of large banks which had strong international links. The nearest example to this type of banking system today is probably Germany. The main advantage of such a system is that the managers and employees who work within this framework are broadly skilled in all aspects of banking.

By 1949 nationalisation meant that virtually all of Hungarian industry was under the control of central and local government. The Communist government developed a system of planning which aimed to integrate productive and distributive activity and thereby influence consumption. Under the nationalisation programme, industrial enterprises were grouped by product and subordinated to the authority of the relevant industrial ministry. In this hierarchical system, all decision making is concentrated at the top, that is enterprises were directed through administrative orders. Any contracts existing between organisations (that is, horizontal links)

77

were made with the knowledge and approval of their mutual superiors. Thus, the means of production were regulated by fiat, that is enterprises were not allowed any choice in technology, markets and so on. Put simply, quantity rationing was almost universal.

4.2 ORGANISATION OF THE BANKING SYSTEM

Although the National Bank of Hungary was by far the largest bank in socialist Hungary, it was not the only bank which operated in this monobank system; more accurately described as a single-tier system. Typically in eastern europe the monobank system does not embody a single bank (Albania being the exception). In a monobank system the central bank is not just the bankers' bank and the lender of last resort, it also maintains ties with various economic units, handling their accounts and carrying out payment orders for them. Thus it has the role of a commercial bank as well as a central bank. In addition to this the central bank grants loans for working capital and some investment. Finally it also manages and carries out foreign currency operations. However, as well as the central bank, there are often one or more investment and/or development banks, which may additionally perform short-term lending operations to a particular industry such as the building industry. The Stalinist model includes a foreign trade bank which shares external operations with the central bank. Each bank is in a monopolistic situation, whether to a certain group of customers, or for certain types of operations such as foreign trade transactions. Finally, various commercial banks exist, but are under the direct control of the central bank.

The banking system was reorganised in 1947 in order to meet the objectives of central planning. The completion of every planned movement of goods and services was to be controlled and monitored by forint (the Hungarian currency). In order to facilitate the adequate movement of goods and services and the payments for them, there was a maximum time lapse before payment of one month. Using an example, the movement of goods from A to B had to be paid for within one month of the receipt of the goods by B. This was viewed as a means of avoiding credit relationships between enterprises, in accordance with Marxist theory. Such a complex system for licensing the movement of goods and services led to an ever greater role for the National Bank of Hungary. The Bank became the centre for all the accounts of state-owned enterprises and for the co-operative sector. Any movement and subsequent payment for goods and services thus required a credit entry in the bank accounts of the enterprises receiving payments of goods and services, and debit entries from those enterprises which had bought the goods and services.

In addition to this complicated system for facilitating the movement of goods and services, the National Bank of Hungary's role expanded to take in all areas of the economy. It remained the bank of issue, and central bank responsible for financing the governments budget deficit. In addition it was a commercial bank, an investment bank for agriculture, one of the major foreign trade banks of the country and the foreign currency management agency. Since the National Bank of Hungary had so many roles, conflicts between them were inevitable. For example, as central bank it was responsible for financing the budget deficit and controlling the money supply, but in its role as a commercial bank (making loans and accepting deposits) it would issue loans to enterprises whose projects appeared profitable in the long term and who also maintained low costs of production. The reality of the National Bank of Hungary's role until the mid 1980s, was that it ceased to operate as a bank of issue, and an efficient commercial bank, but instead financed the targets which were required by the plan. This was achieved by issuing state firms with the necessary capital to invest and meet these planned targets. These state firms were not required to maintain low costs of production or to be profitable. The National Bank of Hungary, although a central bank, did not set any targets for the growth of the money supply or any other aggregate and ignored the size, composition and maturity of bank deposits, thus allowing commercial banks (including itself) to lend to a virtually unlimited extent. That is, commercial banks did not face any liquidity or other constraints.

This lack of liquidity constraints resulted in banks being willing to lend to enterprises without taking account of their profitability and costs of production. This helped to facilitate the "investment hunger" which actually occurred. It resulted in a system whereby loss-making enterprises were rewarded with unlimited credit facilities, even though the likelihood of these loans ever being repaid was minute. The losses of these enterprises were likely to continue well into the future, due to the fact that there were no constraints to force these enterprises to keep their costs under control. The commercial banks did not have to force these firms to maintain low costs as they in turn did not face any liquidity constraints. Meanwhile, small profitable firms which did face competitive constraints were penalised because they were denied access to credit facilities. Thus the single tier banking system operated according to principles which would appear to a western banker as perverse.

The attempts at reform which occurred in Hungary during the late 1960s actually resulted in a more centralised role for the National Bank of Hungary. The aim of these reforms was to introduce the discipline of the market so that the plan would work more efficiently. This new increased role for the National Bank of Hungary was such that the central planning authorities could still exert a considerable influence on preferences, rather than the market constraints of profitability and solvency, thus making the reforms ineffective in the long term. Therefore the monopolistic structure of the National Bank of Hungary acted as a (means to maintain) what remained in reality state-controlled investment and output decisions.

4.3 INVESTMENT FUNDS AND THE COMMUNIST STRUCTURE

Centrally planned economies ration investment funds at a microeconomic level. Each enterprises investment is strictly controlled by the centre in order to fulfil the plan. Kornai (1986) points out that this results in what he described as "Investment Hunger", whereby rewards or investment funds are allocated on the basis of size. Thus the largest firms receive a disproportionately large share of funds for investment purposes. This investment hunger results in bargaining between firms and the central planning authorities about investment resources. Enterprises particularly benefit from the absence of any cost constraints or bankruptcy because the central planning authorities can always be relied on to bail out any loss-making firm in the state sector. The result of this is that state sector firms' actual demand for investment funds is interest-inelastic, because it depends on factors other than the rate of interest, most notably the decisions of central planners.

Moreover, it can be argued that financial intermediation was effected between the household and the firm through the state budget in Hungary, Whereas in market economies this is one of the roles of the commercial (private sector) financial system. Commercial banks bring together the excess funds of households and firms in the form of corporate and personal savings with the demands of firms to borrow for investment purposes at a given price (rate of interest). Financial intermediation was carried out by the state budget in Hungary through the use of wage and price controls and the separation of household and enterprise banking. The only real previous attempt at reforming the communist structure in Hungary occurred during the late 1960s with the introduction of the *New Economic Mechanism*. Although the reforms paid lip service to the ideas of imposing market constraints, in reality they turned out to be yet another version of the Soviet system. The central planning authorities still continued to interfere using taxes and subsidies to influence prices, thereby making any possible market constraints artificial. All the problems of investment hunger remained and arguably actually worsened. This is seen especially clearly when the economy is separated into its main sectors, the state sector and the non-state sector.

The state sector consists of the very large monopolistic state owned enterprises, often the chronic loss makers of Hungarian industry. Belassa (1989) points out that 11 of Hungary's largest firms accounted for approximately 80 per cent of the accumulated losses until 1984. But it is argued, especially by Kornai, that this situation should be expected given the soft budget constraint faced by these enterprises and the paternalistic attitude of the state. Why should the state allow these firms to become insolvent when it was the state who had been responsible for establishing these enterprises in the beginning, so allowing them to go insolvent would effectively admit that the state was wrong to have established them. Thus there was considerable political pressure to keep ailing state-owned enterprises alive and also to support them by allowing these enterprises virtually unlimited access to investment funds.

On the other hand, there is the non-state sector, which includes many co-operatives and licensed private enterprises, mainly in the construction industry. These enterprises were far more profitable, because they faced more competitive pressures. These enterprises found that their profits were very heavily taxed, and that it was virtually impossible to acquire credit for investment purposes. Thus these non-state sector firms were discriminated against for investment purposes. Also they found that the excessive taxes they paid were used to subsidise the chronic loss makers in the state sector. Thus any investment which took place in the non-state sector arose from profits, which had already been reduced substantially as a result of heavy taxation. The Hungarians thus managed a system whereby loss-making enterprises were rewarded with unlimited funds while profit making enterprises were heavily penalised.

4.4 MONETARY POLICY AND THE ROLE OF MONEY

In attempting to change from a planned to market economy, the significance of the role of money and monetary policy must be recognised. Given that in a market economy, money plays the role of integrating all aspects of economic activity, it penetrates every area of economic life. By contrast, a major objective of central planning is to render the role of money and the market superfluous. The idea being that money and markets are replaced by the conscious, systematic guidance of the planning authorities which would provide the framework for peoples' lives and the economy so leading to the age of man's control over social and economic events.

In a market economy, the existence of the integral nature of money and the market mechanism means that money has a number of functions, notably as a measure of value, medium of exchange and a form of accumulation. These functions provide policy making in a market economy with a significant advantage because the economy is easier to analyse. The market system results in an efficient price system where demand and supply are responsive to changes in price, and price is also responsive to the changes in conditions of demand and supply.

Tardos (1989) emphasises that the subordinate role of money in a centrally planned economy results in unsatisfied demand. He argues that the constant systematic guidance of the plan, results in money having a role which is subordinate to the plan. The plan reflects the production targets for various firms. Hence the production of goods becomes an end in itself. Firms have no incentive to respond to consumer preferences and so the changing conditions of demand, instead they aim to produce as many goods as the plan requires, regardless of quality of the good or actual consumer demand for the good. This results in unsatisfied demand, and imbalance between demand and supply, and not to mention a decline in the entrepreneurial spirit.

The Hungarian government's previous attempts at reform, notably around 1968 were aimed at strengthening the price mechanism and the role of money in the economy. It was thought that by doing this prices would now act as a vehicle for the implementation of the plan. Underlying this was the belief that it would create incentives for managers and workers to fulfil the plan effectively. It can be seen from the experience of the 1970s that no market mechanism was really created and that firms were not coordinated by a price mechanism and system of incentives; Kornai (1986), Tardos (1989). Thus the new system of indirect planning did not achieve the breakthrough, of allowing firms to adjust quickly to the changing demands of consumers and of restricting investment to the available savings. Thus the signals that a market mechanism provides to firms and consumers were not developed. By the late 1970s Hungary's trade position had begun to deteriorate as a consequence of the ineffective changes made to the system. As the result of this poor trade position and increasing external debt the Hungarians adopted a restrictive policy of reducing the money supply to reduce income, increase exports and promoting import substitution. Tardos argues that for this type of restrictive monetary policy to improve economic adaptability certain conditions were necessary:

1. The government must be capable of limiting excess demand by the use of fiscal and credit policy.
2. An equilibrium exchange rate.
3. Firms must be induced to react quickly to changes and developments in money markets.
4. Any restructuring of production caused by changes in the conditions of demand and supply must be reflected in prices.
5. Any profitable and/or new activities must have access to funds in order to cover additional wages, raw materials, import costs etc, even when money is tight.
6. Some form of welfare protection for workers who are dismissed as a result of falling demand and cutbacks.

During the period of restraint the government was not prepared to meet any of these pre-conditions. Rather, the policy carried out was that of import restrictions and administrative pressure, hoping that this would boost production and thus keep the economy afloat. Tardos concludes that any financial reforms will only be successful if these reforms, that is, cutting back state investment and the strengthening of credit, are accompanied by the de-regulation of prices, wages and investment, thereby creating an effective signalling mechanism. He also points out the danger of rapid inflation, if these reforms are carried out without a tight control of the growth of effective demand in line with the country's productivity.

If Hungary is to become a market economy there is a strong necessity for an effective monetary policy. The role of monetary policy in a market economy is to make sure that aggregate demand does not exceed productive capacity. In order to be able to carry out an effective monetary policy, the authorities must successfully change the organisation of the banking system from a single-tier to a two-tier banking system. It is generally accepted that for any banking system to be effective in a market economy it must be two-tiered with commercial banks and a separate central bank (preferably controlled or regulated by Parliament). The role of the central bank is to regulate the quantity of money and to finance the government's budget deficit, whilst commercial banks grant loans and accept deposits. The pre-1987 attempts at reform in Hungary harmed efficient firms via the cutting-off (or calling-in) of credits and subsequent increases in interest rates. The result was that those firms turned their backs on the banks, only using their services when forced.

4.5 POST 1987 STRUCTURE AND REFORMS

The establishment of an active capital market should result in a flow of investment funds from low-productivity to high-productivity uses. This will enable firms in difficulty to borrow money in order to improve operations, if and only if the firm has favourable future prospects. It is important to note that commercial banks perform vital functions which make any capital markets operate more efficiently. Their major role is financial intermediation, the acceptance of deposits and the granting of loans. But, for any commercial bank to be efficient it must operate on business principles, that is be a profit maximising institution. It must also face sufficient competition from other financial institutions; the problem of "X-inefficiency" outweighs any monopoly profits. Given the significant role that capital markets and the banking system play in a market economy, the Hungarians altered their banking system on 1 January 1987. Its aim was to create a competitive, two-tier structure, like those in market economies. Essentially, the new structure is the National Bank of Hungary acting only as a central bank, that is it is responsible for regulating the quantity of money and financing the budget deficit. Five large commercial banks, were created together with many smaller institutions (see Table 4.1).

Tardos (1989) argues that certain conditions needed to be met by the Hungarian economy in order to establish an active capital market. Firstly, commercial banks should be free to decide their lending operations, so there must be a very limited role for the state directives. Regulation of the commercial banks to limit the quantity of money in the economy should be through reserve requirements or interest rates. Secondly, banks should be given the right to collect time and savings deposits from whoever they want, that is commercial banks should not be restricted to certain industries or regions. Thirdly, banks should be made fully responsible for the profits and losses of their operations. They must work on business principles and not rely on the state to bail them out if they make losses. Finally, competition is required to ensure that the size of commercial banks is kept fairly small and to avoid specialisation according to a particular industry or region.

Ligetti (in Basckai, 1989) describes four types of banking system which can operate in market economies. Firstly, a system where there is one commercial bank as well as the central bank, this type of banking system faces no competitive pressure due to a monopoly situation. The second type of banking system is where the commercial banks each cover certain geographical regions. The third type is where commercial banks are specialised according to branches or sub branches of the national economy. Types two and three are essentially variants of type one, that is a monopolistic situation, except that the commercial banks are now representatives of particular vested interests, such as a particular industry for example agriculture or a particular region. Finally, the fourth type of system he describes is one where the commercial banks have a

Table 4 1: Banking System in Hungary from January 1987

	Form of Property Rights	Value of Assets in Forints (m)
Central Bank		
National Bank of Hungary	Joint Stock Company	10,000
Commercial Banks		
Hungarian Credit Bank	Joint Stock Company	5,500
National Commercial and Credit Bank	Joint Stock Company	5,500
Budapest Development and Credit Bank	Joint Stock Company	2,500
Hungarian Foreign Trade Bank	Joint Stock Company	3,000
General Assets Trade Bank	Joint Stock Company	1,000
Banks for the Population		
National Savings Bank (OTP)	State Owned	1,300
Development Banks		
State Development Institute	State Owned	
Small Financial Institutions		
Interinvest Foreign Trade Development Association	Deposit Company	2,000
Construction Industry Innovation Bank	Joint Stock Company	744
Agrarian Innovation Bank	Deposit Company	600
Technovia Industrial Innovation Fund	Deposit Company	424
Industrial Co-operative Bank	Deposit Company	300
General Enterprise Bank	Joint Stock Company	2,200
Investment Development Bank	Deposit Company	620
Innofinance General Innovation Fund	Joint Stock Company	500
Banks for Small Businesses	Subsidiary of OTP	300
Hungarian Joint Foreign Banks		
Central European International Bank Ltd, Budapest	Joint Stock Company	$20m (US)
Citibank Budapest	Joint Stock Company	$20m (US)
UNIC Bank	Joint Stock Company	

Source: M.Tardos. E. European Economics, Vol.28, pp.89-90

mixed clientele, that is there are no restrictions placed upon consumers who they bank with, and this provides the bank with the ability to buy expertise, and there is competition amongst banks.

The post 1987 structure in Hungary, although apparently competitive on the surface, was in reality, some combination of Ligetti's types two and three. Commercial banks clienteles were originally divided on an industry basis. Once these restrictions were lifted some enterprises changed banks, so there is some movement towards type four banks with a mixed clientele developing amongst the banks. But, even so, it is difficult to argue that competitive banking conditions exist for a number of reasons. Firstly, and very importantly, the state is the major share holder in the newly formed commercial banks, which are joint stock companies. This leaves room for the state to interfere in the running of the commercial banks, and also a feeling amongst the banks that the state can be relied to bail them out if things go wrong. Thus these commercial banks are not yet operating on truly competitive business principles. Secondly, the state still provides capital subsidies to enterprises. It is therefore difficult to imagine that the new banks will operate on strict business principles, that is lending to clients will become "hard". Unless the banks are willing recall loans from loss-making firms, (thus bankrupting the loss-making firm) it is difficult to envisage a proper business relationship between the bank and firm developing. Finally, commercial banks differ significantly in size, strength and branch networks and also regulation by the National Bank of Hungary on interest charges, the re-financing of credits and reserve requirements.

Essentially, the banking system was restructured in 1987, to enable an easier transformation to a market economy and to create some form of market mechanism. It was believed that the changes would encourage the decentralisation of investment decisions of enterprises, by linking the investment decision to the profitability of the particular enterprise. Secondly, it was thought that it would provide incentives for Hungarian savings to go to efficient industries, that is, to ensure the movement of funds from low profitability activities to high profitability activities. The real interest rate on savings deposits in Hungary has been traditionally negative, whilst the interest rate paid on bonds is much higher. Typically there is a tax free interest rate of approximately 11 per cent pa on bonds, whilst only between 3 and 7 percent is paid on savings deposits. It is a moot point whether such encouragement of the bond market is desirable. Belassa (1989) argues that it is. He points out that one method of encouraging firms to use profits efficiently, would be to increase bond issues, thereby establishing an even more active capital market. This has been encouraged because firms have been granted autonomy over their after-tax profits, that is, they can now choose to invest them in the area where they will get the highest rate of return. Thus, any rational firm will purchase bonds where the rate of return is higher, rather than save their excess income in a commercial bank where they receive a negative rate of return.

4.6 THE HUNGARIAN STOCK EXCHANGE

The Hungarians opened their stock exchange in June 1990. It opened with only 42 members initially; many of these original members are joint ventures with Hungarian firms, such as Citibank Budapest which is 80 percent owned by Citibank New York. The stock exchange is very small, the founding members and their basic capital are shown in Table 4.2. Essentially there are two types of firms listed on the stock exchange. The first type applied to smaller firms, who need only have 5 million forints of original capital to establish a joint stock company. These firms must be registered in Hungary, Very importantly, the rules of the stock exchange do not prohibit any stock exchange firm being founded with wholly foreign ownership, which is the case with firms owned by Girozentrale and Handerbank both German banks. It is also possible according to the rules of the stock exchange to have self-employed single person broker firms, although it is generally accepted that it would be difficult for a broker to earn enough from broking to be employed full time. Alternatively, larger firms require a minimum of 50 million Forints of original capital. With the rules applying to smaller and larger firms are however, the same.

It is difficult to envisage why the Hungarians opened the atock exchange, without actually having the profit-making firms needed to be traded on it. The Hungarians were faced with a dilemma of whether to create the classic market institution; a stock exchange without having the markets for it to rely on. This is often described by market economists as the Industry-Infrastructure debate. That is which is more important, or

Table 4.2: Founding Members of Budapest Stock Exchange June 1990.

Name	Basic Capital (Ft)
Agrobank Ltd	1.5 bn
General Bank and Trust Company Ltd	1 bn
Anker Securities Inc	50 m
General Venture Finance Bank Ltd	2.205 bn
Budapest Bank Ltd	6.585 bn
CA-BB Brokers Ltd	50 m
Citibank Budapest Ltd	1 bn
Co-Nexus Corporation	53 m
Duna Investment and Commercial Bank Co Ltd	1 bn
First American Bank of Hungary	1 bn
First American-Hungarian Securities Ltd	50 m
First Hungarian-English Broker Agency	5.1 bn
First German Securities Ltd in Hungary	50 m
Innovative Centre (Park) Share Company of North Hungary	147 m
YBL Bank for Building Innovation Industry	1.160 bn
Economic Consultant Ltd	5 m
General Broker Ltd	9 m
Girozentrale Investment Ltd	100 m
Real Estate Bank Ltd	840 m
General Finance Institution for Innovation Ltd	500 m
Inter-Europa Bank	2.807 bn
Investment Technical Development Bank Ltd	1.245 bn
Investtrade Ltd	6.307 bn
Industrial Development Ltd	1.06 bn
Industrial Co-operative Development Bank Ltd	3.2 bn
Consumer Co-operatives Bank Ltd	962 m
Central-European Bank	1 bn
Central-European Brokers Ltd	5 m
Kulturbank Ltd	1 bn
Landerbank Broker Budapest Ltd	50 m
Hungarian Credit Bank	14 bn
Hungarian Foreign Trade Bank Ltd	6.003 bn
Bank of Hungarian Savings Co-operatives Ltd	1.035 bn
MID Broker Ltd	5 m
Agricultural Co-operatives Company Ltd	2.3608 bn
Nordline Corp.	
National Bank of Hungary	
Post Bank and Savings Bank Corporation	2.229 bn
Rotter and Co Hungarian Broker House Ltd	50 m
Szenzor Broker Ltd	5 m
Commercial and Credit Bank Ltd	12.59 bn

Source: Hungarian Trade Journal, Sept 1990 Vol.40 No.9

should be created first, the market system of free prices, wages, entrepreneurial spirit and profit maximising firms or the institutions such as the stock market which might act as an incentive to create the market system.

The Hungarians established the stock exchange for a number of reasons, firstly, as a result of the belief that an under-developed market was better than none at all, and that it would provide additional help to the process of development and the movement towards a market economy. A second reason for establishing the stock exchange would be to encourage foreign investment in Hungary, this is given a further fillip with the liberal rules of the stock exchange, particularly, the encouragement of wholly foreign owned firms establishing themselves as Joint Stock Companies with a quotation on the Budapest Stock Exchange. Naturally, with foreign investment there often comes expertise in market techniques, efficiency, profit motivation and competition. Thus the aim is to use the Stock Exchange as an incentive to be profitable, to force competition upon firms and thus eventually these firms will be privatised and appear on the Stock Exchange list.

Much of the evidence of foreign investment into Hungary is indicated by the large number of joint ventures which have been enacted, for example, there were over 1000 new joint ventures in 1990. Although most of these were small firms, there were numerous large joint ventures such as Citibank Budapest mentioned previously, Central European International Bank, and the Long Term Credit Bank of Japan on the finance side of the economy. Whilst in manufacturing there have been numerous investments, notably General Electric purchasing 50 per cent of Tungstram Ltd Hungary, whilst Ford and Suzuki are both building plants.

4.7 SUMMARY AND CONCLUSIONS

The Hungarians have gradually set about reforming the financial sector of their economy. Firstly, they have begun the difficult task of creating competitive banking conditions by creating a free market framework for their banking system, that is creating separate central banking and commercial banking institutions. Although these institutions are still state-owned in the main, their roles and objectives are now much clearer, than under the previous system.

The introduction of the Stock Exchange in 1990, is to be regarded as a signal to overseas investors about the seriousness that the Hungarians are taking the move towards a market economy. Undoubtedly its establishment will encourage overseas investment into the economy, and also encourage the necessary expertise and skills that a market economy requires to maintain these necessary market institutions, required for the successful movement towards a market economy.

Unfortunately, serious problems remain, the vast majority of enterprises are still state-owned and unprofitable. Only the process of privatisation and the creation of a large substantial private sector will eliminate this problem. The establishment of the stock exchange is aimed at helping this, thus when a state owned enterprise becomes profitable it will be privatised by selling its shares through the stock exchange. But it is difficult to envisage how rapidly the privatisation process will proceed with so many enterprises making losses. Secondly, the economy is still cushioned from world markets because of the inconvertibility of the forint and protection to home producers from foreign competitors who would undoubtedly be able to undercut their prices because they are cost effective producers unlike the Hungarian firms. The large Hungarian enterprises are facing only a gradual hardening of their cost constraint because how they affect other sectors of the economy. The financial sector will be more than willing to allow enterprises to repay their debts gradually, because otherwise they would face a very large debt problem, which would result in both enterprises and banks becoming insolvent, also consumers are facing ever increasing unemployment and inflation which could quickly lead to discontent and disillusionment, with the reforms taking place.

The creation of a "competitive" banking system and a stock exchange reflect enthusiasm for market economy institutions and procedures, which compares with the Polish experience, even though they are very different. Whilst the Polish have opted for the market system without the institutions, by freeing all prices during the last year. The Hungarians have decided to act differently by establishing the institutions hoping that it will act as an incentive to a market system, with free prices, wages and profit maximising firms.

91

92 - 121

5 The development of monetary policy instruments in Poland

Wieslaw Kalinowski and
Wieslaw Zoltkowski

Poland
P34 P21
E52

5.1 AN OVERALL VIEW

In order to understand recent developments in monetary policy in Poland, it is necessary to look backwards to the period of central economic planning in Poland, during which money played only a minor role. During that period the function of money as a planning instrument was changing. In the 1980s the relationship between flows of money and the exchange of goods became considerably closer, and monetary conditions became less vulnerable to the effects of arbitrary decisions by the political authorities. Nevertheless, until 1988 the National Bank of Poland (NBP) was not only the central bank but also the main credit and deposit bank—the "monobank"—in Poland. It was in that year that a major programme of reform of the banking system began; as part of the programme, the range of functions of the NBP was greatly reduced, its main functions being limited to the following:

- central bank of the state
- note issuing bank
- banker to the banking system.

In addition, nine large commercial state banks were established to take over the functions of former operational regional branches of the NBP. The areas served by these banks overlap, so that there is some limited competition. New banks proliferated in 1990, when 49 licences were granted for the establishment of commercial banks (30 of which are predominantly owned by private shareholders). At present there are 79 state and privately-owned banks in Poland; in addition there are 1,650 co-operative banks, most of which are agricultural banks. Most of the private banks are very small.

During 1988 and 1989, following the change in the functions of the NBP, policy instruments designed to influence bank behaviour and implement monetary policy were developed, as follows:

- Commercial banks were made subject to the obligation to hold reserves at the NBP.
- Commercial banks were offered access to refinancing credit in order to support their lending. The total amount of refinancing credit was determined by macroeconomic policy considerations; within the total, each bank's share was determined by reference to its financial situation. The conditions under which refinancing credits were available were set out in agreements between the NBP and each of the large commercial banks. In the event of a bank borrowing beyond its share, the sanctions available to the NBP included increasing the interest rate on the credit, and restriction of credit.

Until the end of 1989, some categories of borrowing from banks were eligible for concessionary interest rates. These loans were refinanced by the NBP and the cost of the interest rate subsidy was borne by the state budget.

At the beginning of 1990 Poland began the implementation of the economic programme worked out in co-operation with the IMF. The main objectives of the programme were:

- to bring down inflation and restore macroeconomic balance;
- to strengthen the role of the national currency;
- to make the national currency convertible for foreign trade settlements;

93

- to initiate the process of privatisation and the restructuring of the economy.

The main task of the NBP, as the institution responsible for monetary policy, was to be to regulate the growth of the money supply in order to contain aggregate demand and control the rate of price increase. To this end, a number of steps were taken at the beginning of 1990:

1   A positive real interest rate, protecting deposits and savings against the consequences of inflation, was established.
2   The previous arrangements for preferential interest rates for particular categories of lending were largely abandoned, though preferential rates were retained for some types of lending.
3   The problem which arose from bank loans which had been taken out at a low fixed interest rate when the price level was much lower was settled.
4   The NBP was no longer permitted to lend to the government.
5   The exchange rate of the Polish zloty was devalued to a level ($1 = zl9,500) at which there was a balance between supply and demand in the foreign exchange market.

In this new environment, the NBP's main concerns were with the money supply, interest rate policy and foreign exchange rate policy. At the beginning of 1990, a macroeconomic adjustment programme was put into effect, including devaluation of the zloty, a rise in interest rates to previously unheard-of levels, and deep cuts in subsidies. Despite the difficult economic conditions in which monetary policy had to be implemented in 1990, positive results began to appear fairly quickly. The Government succeeded in curbing hyperinflation and containing aggregate demand to a level roughly balancing the productive capacity of the economy. The Polish zloty became internally convertible and as a result, the national currency was in a general sense much more highly valued by the people. A foreign trade surplus emerged. The demonopolisation of the economy began, and proceeded most rapidly in domestic and foreign trade.

On the other hand there were also some negative results. There was a sharp decline in internal demand; measured output fell by about 30 per cent from the levels of a year earlier and unemployment began to increase fast. Real money supply fell by about a third in the first quarter of 1990, but began to rise again and increased by 17 per cent in the second and third quarters. This led to an upturn in inflation and provoked a tightening in monetary policy in the latter part of the year.

In general, however, the implementation of monetary policy in 1990 was successful. With the exchange rate of the zloty against the US dollar steady, the national currency became the main medium of exchange. The share of zloty deposits in M_3 (which also includes foreign currency deposits) increased from 22 per cent in December 1989 to over 56 per cent in June 1991. Interest rates were kept consistently positive in real terms by appropriate management by the NBP of the interest rate on refunding credit, preferential interest rates for particular types of credit having been largely abandoned.

The monetary policy of the NBP was guided in part by the development of the money supply: the NBP aimed to maintain a stable relationship between money supply and the nominal value of Gross Product. The NBP aimed to influence not only the cost but also the accessibility of money, with the help of a number of monetary policy instruments. In the early part of 1990, obligatory reserve ratios applied to banks were increased, and banks' access to refunding credit was subjected to limits. Later in the year, direct controls on credit were imposed; at the same time, the NBP began to issue short-term bills by regular auction to absorb surplus liquidity from the banking system. Later the Treasury also began to issue bills for budget financing purposes. Interest rate policy. The main role in implementing interest rate policy is played by the refinancing credit rate fixed by the NBP. The relationship between the refinancing credit rate and the monthly increase in the index of retail prices of goods and services during 1990 and early 1991 is given in the appendix to Chapter 6. This shows how, as the rate of inflation fell after the beginning of 1990, so interest rates also fell, broadly in parallel.

From September 1990, however, the inflation rate went back up to the range 4.6–5.9 per cent a month. In response, the interest rate on refinancing credit was increased in October. That increase proved to be inadequate to halt the rise in inflation, and there were further increases in November 1990 and February 1991; the latter took the interest rate on refinancing credit up to 72 per cent

In the new environment, commercial banks were able to determine interest rates on credits and deposits autonomously. The NBP however recommended to state banks the rates they should charge for credits to reliable borrowers, as well as minimum rates on deposits. The abandonment of preferential interest rates on credits was not complete, and notable exceptions in 1990 were the financing of housing, and of food reserves, where there were (in the former case) mandatory partial capitalisation of interest and (in both cases) interest subsidies from the budget. Poland still has a very large state sector which is of course not directly affected by variations in interest rates; and in some parts of the private sector (though by no means all) profit margins are so wide that interest rate-related receipts and payments are not of primary importance. Nevertheless interest rate changes did appear to come to affect monetary growth and to influence the rate of inflation.

5.2 INSTRUMENTS OF MONETARY POLICY

Obligatory reserves

Obligatory reserve ratios were increased steadily during the course of 1990 in order to help absorb the increase in bank liquidity which arose primarily from a rise in foreign exchange reserves. The calculation of each bank's obligatory reserves is based on its deposit balances at the end of the preceding month.

The average obligatory reserve ratio changed as follows:

From:		
	31 December 1989	10 percent
	30 March 1990	9 percent
	30 April 1990	15 percent
	31 August 1990	21 percent
	31 October 1990	22 percent
	31 December 1990	24 percent

Obligatory reserves played an essential role in absorbing surplus liquidity from the banking system and limiting the growth of money supply. Nevertheless non-interest-bearing obligatory reserves distort banks' asset management decisions and represent an imperfect instrument for this purpose.

Open market operations

In July 1990 the NBP added to its techniques for managing banking system liquidity the issue of short-term bills which are fairly tradeable. These bills are liabilities of the NBP. They are non-interest bearing instruments sold at a discount to their face value–that is, their value at maturity. They are sold at weekly tenders organised by the NBP, are available in denominations of Zl 100 million, Zl 1,000 million and Zl 10,000 million. The bills issued initially were for a maturity of 30 days; those currently in issue have maturities of 28, 91 and 182 days: variations in the size of the NBP bill issue have immediate effects on the liquidity of the banking system.

The tender procedure is as follows. Bids are sent on special forms to NBP headquarters and compared (by computer) on Thursdays at 12 noon. Bills are sold to those tenderers who offer the highest price–stated in zlotys for each Zl 100 nominal of bills–until the pre-set amount of bills on offer has been exhausted. Once made, bids for bills are binding on the bidder. Tenderers are notified of the NBP's response to their bids on the day after the auction, when the result is also published in the daily newspaper *"Rzeczpospolita"*. Settlement of the tender–that is, the exchange of bills for money—takes place on the Monday after the auction; each successful bidder takes delivery and pays for bills at his local NBP branch. Holders of NBP bills have the option of selling them in the market before maturity, or of selling them back to the NBP before maturity. The NBP announces each week with the result of the weekly tender the discount rate at which it will repurchase NBP bills.

In 1990 there were 22 NBP bill tenders, at which the NBP offered for sale Zl 21.4 trillion worth of bills. Total bids amounted to Zl 19.7 trillion—that is, 92 per cent of the amount offered. Some of these bids were however at tenders which were oversubscribed, and some were at discount rates unacceptable to the NBP, and the total of bills sold at tenders was Zl 15.7 billion—that is, 73 per cent of the amount offered. The average discount rate was 37 per cent. In the first five months of 1991, there were 22 tenders, at which Zl 16.4 trillion of bills were offered for sale. Total bids were Zl 21.3 trillion (129.9 percent of the amount offered), and the amount sold at the tenders was Zl 12.5 trillion (68.8 per cent).

The sale of NBP bills helped to limit the liquid monetary reserves of the banking system. The value of bills in circulation was as follows:

31 August 1990	Zl 1.6083 trillion
30 September 1990	Zl 3.2145 trillion
31 October 1990	Zl 3.8071 trillion
30 November 1990	Zl 2.6431 trillion
31 December 1990	Zl 0.5002 trillion
31 January 1991	Zl 2.5389 trillion
28 February 1991	Zl 2.4996 trillion
31 March 1991	Zl 2.1203 trillion
30 April 1991	Zl 3.9847 trillion
31 May 1991	Zl 1.8563 trillion

During this period banks' total liquid reserves were in the range Zl 14–18 trillion, so that 10–20 perecent of liquid reserves were held in the form of NBP bills.

In May 1991, the Ministry of Finance began the issue of Treasury bills, which are liabilities of the government, not of the NBP (though the NBP acts as the issuing agent). In other respects they are similar to NBP bills; and the method of sale is also similar. The NBP acts as the issuing agent. Their purpose is to raise funds for the state budget (as already indicated, the NBP is not allowed to lend to the government). The Budget Act allows the Minister of Finance to issue up to Zl 30 trillion of Treasury bills in 1991; the amount outstanding may not exceed Zl 4.1763 trillion. In May 1991, some Zl 2.7 trillion worth of Treasury bills with 4 and 8 weeks to maturity were offered for sale. Total bids at the tenders were Zl 2.5826 trillion, and total sales Zl 2.0533 trillion.

Investment income is taxed in Poland at a rate of 40 per cent, but income from NBP bills and Treasury bills is exempt from this tax. Accordingly the return on these bills, compared to the return on other assets, is much more attractive than a crude comparison of yields would suggest. The tables on p.121 show how the yields struck at bill tenders have compared with the interest rate on refinancing credit.

98

5.3 THE DEVELOPMENT OF A SECONDARY MARKET

In an attempt to stimulate the development of a money market and in particular to facilitate secondary turnover of NBP bills and Treasury bills, the NBP has established a broking service in bills. The principles of the business are as follows:

- clients interested in buying or selling bills notify their bids and offers to the NBP;
- the NBP provides customers with information about bids and offers, matches buyers with sellers and makes arrangements for negotiating a deal;
- when the deal has been struck, the NBP facilitates settlement by instructing those of its branches which are located closest to the two parties to the deal to accept the bills from the seller and pay him the funds due, and accept payment from the buyer and issues the bills to him;
- settlement takes place on the second business day after the deal is struck.

The NBP makes no charge for this intermediation, which is intended as a means of promoting secondary market activity. Turnover thus far has been limited, however, reflecting lack of interest thus far among the major banks in trading bills.

The NBP has now abandoned the practice of providing refinancing credit to banks up to pre-set limits. Instead, it is now offering to provide funds to the banks in the following ways:

- rediscount credit—that is, rediscounting bills of exchange which the bank has accepted.
- Lombard credit—that is, short-term loans against the collateral of securities pledged by the bank.
- auctions of sale and repurchase agreements with the NBP.

The regulation issued on 31 January 1989 reintroduced bills of exchange into Poland after a long absence. Banks now have the right to discount bills, and the NBP is willing to rediscount bills discounted by other banks. Initially, in order to promote the use of bills, the NBP set the interest rate on rediscount credit at a level lower than the rate on refinancing credit, and as a result, the amount of bills discounted rose rapidly during 1990, as did the amount rediscounted by the NBP. By 1991, bills of exchange had been successfully re-established in Poland, and in order to help restrain monetary growth the NBP set a limit to the amount of bills discounted by each bank that it was prepared to rediscount, the limit being set at 20 per cent of each bank's capital and reserves.

Lombard credit is extended to banks against the collateral of NBP bills, Treasury bills and bills of exchange. The facility has however not been widely used as yet.

The auction of sale and repurchase agreements with the NBP is a recent innovation. Auctions are held each week for sale and repurchase agreements with a maturity of 14 days. Banks participating in the auctions state the value of the securities they are offering for sale and repurchase and the interest rate they are prepared to pay for the funds they will receive.

In the nine auctions held between 23 April and 18 June 1991, the NBP offered to purchase some Zl 1.3 trillion of securities. Total offers were Zl 1.187 trillion, and total sales were Zl 0.764 trillion, or 58.77 percent of the amount the NBP offered to purchase. The interest rate struck at the auctions fluctuated between 59.66 per cent and 73.29 per cent.

6 The Polish experience:

the financial system, economic development, and macroeconomic policies in post-communist countries[*]

Zbigniew Polanski

Poland

P34 P21

101 - 121

E 6

6.1 INTRODUCTION

The dramatic social, economic, and political events that are taking place in eastern europe have still not produced substantial modifications in the structure and performance of their financial systems. The rudimentary financial sector continue to be one of the important elements of the general absence the infra-structure of a market system. In economic theory the significance of financial markets, banks and other financial institutions in the economic development of market economies is often stressed. The rise in the importance of financial institutions in the transition process to a market economy is obvious if we realize that money and finance are essentially a substitute for economic centralization.

[*] This is a revised version of a paper presented at "The Polish-American Conference on the Political Economy of the Transition from Communism" organized by the Center for the Study of Post-Communist Societies, University of Maryland, College Park, December 3–5, 1990. I would like to express gratitude to Bartöomiej Kamiúski for his help and encouragement, to Douglas Poole for language assistance and to Ryszard Kokoszczyúski for his comments. Needless to say, however, that I am the only person responsible for the remaining errors.

6.2 ECONOMIC MANAGEMENT AND THE FINANCIAL SYSTEM IN THE CLASSICAL COMMUNIST ECONOMY

The workings and structure of the communist economy were the effect of an attempt to build up a system based on a direct management of physical resources. Its functioning was founded on bureaucratic regulation, which in turn was strongly linked to the state ownership of the means of production. As a result the financial system and monetary flows were assigned virtually no functions other than passive accountancy and control of real economic processes taking place in state-owned enterprises.

The role assigned to the financial system had a decisive influence in shaping its institutional framework. The financial system had a very simple structure. Its main part – the banking sector – was based on the idea of a monobank, that is, an institution which was performing the functions of both commercial banks and of a central bank. Of course, in practice, in every communist economy there was more than one banking institution. Nevertheless, the basic principles of the monobank idea were always preserved. The banking system was based on the principle that each agent had access to only one bank; the activities of every bank (and even its branches) were strictly assigned to specific spheres of the economy and, therefore, no competition existed.

The absence of factors which could stimulate the development of financial markets led to a very restricted variety of financial assets in the economy. Essentially, the only financial asset was money, in the form of cash and deposits (book money). There were no other – domestic and legal at the same time – financial assets. As a result the finances of state-owned enterprises were based on three sources: internal accumulation (profits from sale of the products and services), budgetary subsidies, and bank credits. The proportions of financing from these three sources changed from country to country and over time. Nevertheless, the current functioning of enterprises was always mainly based on working-capital bank credits. In order to make the enterprises more dependent on bank control state owned-enterprises were given an inadequate quantity of money to run the current production without the use of bank credit.

The absence of financial markets and commercial banks resulted also in the lack of economic (non-administrative) instruments to control the money supply. It was possible (at least to a certain extent) to decelerate the rise in the money supply only by administrative (bureaucratic) methods such as the imposition of ceilings on bank lending activities. In theory a rise in the interest on bank loans could have been used to hamper the demand for them. In practice, however, this did not reduce the demand for credit, as state-owned enterprises lacked hard budget constraints and there was no stimulus to increase profits and lower the costs of production. In fact, in this system, there was no place for a traditional monetary policy; there was only room for a passive credit policy. Under such circumstances the central bank in the communist economy, that is, in practice the largest bank, was not a bankers' bank (as in market economies), but was merely an enterprises' bank.

The financial system under consideration was not designed to perform the function of intermediation between surplus and deficit economic units, and, therefore, to transform saving into investment. As a result the financial system neither stimulated an increase in the rate of savings, nor influenced the allocation of financial resources to investment projects. Under the bureaucratic co-ordination mechanism the level of investment was independent from economic units' voluntary savings, and the level (as well as the structure) of investment was decided by political bodies or by the Central Planning Board without taking into account the financial aspects of the projects.

The role assigned to monetary flows and the financial system in the command economy created certain peculiar properties that are non-existent in other financial systems, especially in fully-developed market economies. First, the functioning and the structure of the financial system was not directed to stimulate the dynamics of economic development. In the command economy it was assumed that this would be accomplished by selective policies imposed through government management based on real variables. Second, the financial system was essentially constructed to perform only an accommodating monetary (credit) policy, mainly because its primitive and highly formalized structure not only did not develop economic instruments to control the money supply but also led to many rigidities and, thus, to the absence of flexible channels of transmission for financial policy. This meant that the financial system was one of the important sources of excess demand in the communist economy, leading therefore to a permanent state of shortages in the markets.

The financial system outlined above existed in nearly unchanged from until the end of the 1980s in all East European (except Yugoslavia) countries. It is true that during the whole decade some modifications were made in corporate finance and some countries like Hungary(1987) and Poland(1989), began to build a two-tier banking system. Nonetheless, despite this modifications, the logic of the financial system did not essentially change.

6.3 THE GREAT INCONSISTENCY AND ITS ESSENCE

The post-communist societies are now facing the task of moving away from the present economic system, which retains elements of the old bureaucratic mechanism, to a system based essentially on a market co-ordinating mechanism. Money and financial institutions play a key role in regulating the functioning, and stimulating the growth of, market oriented systems. However, the financial system cannot be modified in the short run. The creation of a flexible and well-tuned financial system will require a long time. The emergence of a well developed and efficient financial system is connected to the existence of a complex financial structure and often highly complicated regulatory framework, which change in an evolutionary way. These changes by nature take a long time.

Nevertheless, virtually all east european countries are trying now to eliminate the remaining elements of the bureaucratic co-ordination mechanism. As the modifications in the financial system have had to lag behind in these attempts to move to a market economy, the post-communist societies are facing a basic problem: how to manage the economic system according to the logic of a market economy (that is, by monetary and fiscal tools), while at the same time ensuring a decent level of economic growth and an appropriate balance of supply and demand. To what extent is it possible, under existing institutional framework, to conduct market-type macroeconomic policies, securing simultaneously growth and stability?

It is well known that the financial system in a market economy performs both macro- and microeconomic functions. At the macroeconomic level it enhances saving and mediates between the surplus units and deficit spending units looking for sources of investment. Another macroeconomic function of the financial system is to provide a framework to supply the necessary quantity of money for smooth economic development. At the microeconomic level the role of the financial system is to ensure an optimal allocation of money resources, that is, to uses yielding the highest rate of return. The financial system in a market economy plays an active role in this selection process. Finally, the financial system administers the payment mechanism between economic agents. The efficient performance of all these functions by the financial system leads to the reduction of the transaction costs of economic development and, therefore, increase the opportunities for growth.

A financial system whose structure and properties are directed to perform only passive accountancy and control functions is not equipped to conduct the tasks performed by a financial system in a market economy. Therefore, the financial systems inherited by post-communist societies are not suitable to harmonize efficiently the functioning of an economic system based on market-coordination principles. In other words, between the institutional structure of the financial system and its properties and the requirements of the new economic system there is a basic inconsistency. This inconsistency already distorts the current economic policy and will negatively influence the long-term economic development of post-communist countries.

More precisely, the principal spheres of the inconsistency between the anachronistic financial system and an economic system based on market co-ordination includes the following major points. As mentioned above the inherited financial system cannot stimulate an increase in saving, which is vital in the situation of a general lack of capital and a great demand for it caused by the need to restructure the real sphere of the economy during the transition process. Moreover, the allocative efficiency of the banking sector and capital markets do not develop overnight. Thus, even though the administrative mechanism for balancing investment with saving was abolished, it is doubtful whether the financial system can actively and smoothly transform saving into investment. Under these circumstances the economic development of post-communist countries must have a propensity to low and uneven dynamic, and to strong inflationary or deflationary tendencies. The latter will also result from the absence of economic instruments which enable a relatively exact control of the money supply.

However, the highest degree of tension between the anachronistic financial system and the needs of a market economy must take place in the period of changing from one co-ordination mechanism to another. The departure from the bureaucratic mechanism, that is, the increase of the autonomy in the decision making by state-owned enterprises, combined with a passive financial system threatens a sharp destabilization of the economy, evidenced by the intensification of both open and suppressed inflation, and in consequence by a decline in the economic growth performance. On the other hand, under the anachronistic financial system, the introduction of a highly restrictive economic policy to stabilize the economy by raising the banking interest rate and introducing ceilings on extended credits inevitably leads to recession and only a limited success in combating inflation.

6.4 THE POLISH EXPERIENCES

At the threshold of the 1990s decade former communist countries have been in the first of the above mentioned situations as confirmed by their strong suppressed inflation and growth problems. Until now only a few post-communist countries have really began the second phase on the road to a market economy. From this point of view the Polish case is uniquely interesting. First, in only two years (1989-1990) two opposite economic policies were introduced to speed up the process of marketization. Second, the clash between the existing financial system, the adopted macroeconomic policy, and economic development has been particularly visible in Poland.

Attempts at Marketization by the Communist Governments

Poland had already in 1982 attempted to abandon the traditional bureaucratic economic system in the direction of what J. Kornai called "reform socialism". One of the basic features of this economic reform was an absence of major changes in the financial system, although some modifications in corporate finance as well as in the price and tax systems took place.

In order to reduce the inflationary pressure efforts were made to conduct a tight monetary policy by placing ceilings on bank credits for working-capital extended to state-owned enterprises . In the 1980s such a policy was introduced twice: from mid 1983 until mid 1985, and in 1987. This credit policy did not reduce inflation as enterprises in the first instance always financed wages and postponed the repayments of credits (and also of taxes). More importantly, enterprises reacted to this restrictive credit policy by creating "chains of insolvency", As inter-firm trade credit which spilled over the whole socialized sector. The possibility of creating such credit on a wide scale was the result of the logic of the financial system. The assumption of the basic role of real flows in the economic process as well as the low level of working capital in state-owned enterprises induced – when attempts to decelerate the rise of credit supply became effective – the enterprises to operate on a trade credit basis. The possibility of creation of such credit enabled the enterprises not to perform any major adjustments towards efficiency. Thus, credit policy, in the existing institutional framework, was not capable of restricting inflation nor of speeding up the allocative process.

This policy of administrative restriction on bank credits also had a certain – although difficult to estimate exactly – negative impact on the volume of goods produced. Under the conditions of economics of shortage this fact persuaded the authorities to relax their initially tight credit policies.

These negative results of an active use of credit policy to ensure macroeconomic stability as well as to expand the role of market mechanisms in Polish economy were one of the factors that pushed the communist authorities to make changes in the financial structure of the economy. In the 1987-1989 period the National Bank of Poland was segmented, and a two-tier banking system was legally introduced. Also, already in the Autumn of 1987, primary issues of securities (by state-owned enterprises) were permitted. Nonetheless, despite these attempts to develop the financial sector it remained outdated and incapable of stimulating the development of market mechanisms and controlling the rising inflation.

The above problems with achieving economic stability and stimulating economic development were symptoms of the inconsistency described in the previous section. The rigid and rudimentary financial system distorted a macroeconomic policy which neither stopped inflation nor enabled robust economic growth. As a consequence, the last communist government, which took power in the Autumn of 1988, introduced an economic policy which attempted to bypass the existing inconsistency between the financial system, restrictive credit policy, and economic development. In order to stimulate the economic growth and the rise of the private sector, both central planning and bureaucratic constraints on private activity were abolished. Simultaneously, control on credit lending activities was almost completely relaxed. Under these circumstances the cessation of the use of bureaucratic instruments to co-ordinate the economy led to a sharp rise in the inflation rate. A liberalization of food prices combined with a freeze of subsidies in the agricultural sector, in the circumstances of its monopolistic structure, led in August 1989 – in the absence of any monetary control – to hyperinflation.

The result of this attempt to bypass the outlined inconsistency proved to be unsuccessful not only because it led to a sharp rise in the inflation rate but also because recessionary tendencies appeared. In 1989 the volume of the national income did not practically increase.

The 1990 Stabilization Effort

The collapse of the above policy, especially the development of hyperinflation, encouraged the adoption of a radically different policy. The new non-communist government, under the pressure of international financial institutions and in the absence of major alternative programmes by Polish economists, as well as in the face of great social expectations concerning the quick reduction in the inflation rate, adopted an orthodox stabilization programme as a key element for economic policy in 1990.

According to this programme all remaining elements of bureaucratic co-ordination should be abolished simultaneously, that is, the programme assumed that the stabilization of the economy and its latter development would take place practically without any direct state intervention. As one of the architects of the programme put it: "The revival will come by itself." Consequently, the programme focused mainly on non-selective macroeconomic policies. Monetary and fiscal measures, together with incomes policy (which was essentially a derivative of fiscal policy) and rate of exchange policy were the main pillars of the programme for 1990. According to the Letter of Intent sent by Polish Authorities to the International Monetary Found (December 1989), it was expected that tight macroeconomic measures, coupled with liberalization, would cause the inflation rate to decline to 1 per cent (on a monthly basis) in six months, and lead to the appearance of allocative mechanism that would later induce economic growth. In general, the logic of the 1990 economic programme assumed that stabilization macropolicies should have priority while institutional changes ought to take place after stabilization was achieved. As a result the inconsistency between the existing institutional framework, the economic policy, and economic development appeared rampant.

In 1990 monetary policy for the first time since the Second World War became of primary importance in Polish government's economic policy. Moreover it was in the field of monetary policy that the main forms of the inconsistency appeared.

The key characteristic of this policy was its rigorousness. In face of the practical non-existence of financial markets, only the interest rates on bank credits, reinforced additionally by credit ceilings, could be used to stop the growth of money supply. Thus a policy of a high (real positive) interest rate was adopted. It was gradually – on a monthly basis during the first half of the year – lowered in relation to changes in the inflation rate.

Another important feature of the 1990 monetary policy was a nearly absolute (particularly in the first half of the year) withdrawal from selective credit policies. As mentioned, this was an element of a wider economic strategy: also tax exemptions were abolished and subsidies were further cut.

However, despite the introduction at the beginning of 1990 of a package of systemic changes in the economy's mechanisms, monetary policy essentially continue to be a credit policy. Although formally the monobank no longer existed, in practice the main tool of the central bank to control the credit expansion continued to be the interest rates on loans extended by nominally independent (in theory) commercial banks. This was achieved through "moral suasion". Its use was facilitated by the fact that the largest Polish commercial banks were created as a result of partition of the National Bank of Poland (they remained state-owned).

Attempts were also made to utilize instruments more typical for central bank management in market economies. However, in the absence of developed financial markets, only one instrument could be used more actively, that is, changes in the reserve requirement ratios. In order to decrease the banks' excessive liquidity these ratios were changed several times during 1990.

Both ways of controlling the money supply, that is, moral suasion and the increase of reserve requirement ratios, had a negative impact on the performance of the financial system by inducing additional uncertainty and hampering the development of financial markets. Moreover, they proved to be to a great extent ineffective: already in mid 1990 the rise in the increase of the money supply (M2) was higher than planned for the whole year, thus allowing the prices to rise much more than intended. However, this rise of the money supply was not only the result of the credit expansion but was mainly linked to the (unexpected by the government) large trade surplus.

Nonetheless, the 1990 monetary policy was an important attempt to withdraw from the automatic and very selective credit policies led by previous governments, in the absence of a suitable economic and institutional framework. How then did the economy react to such a policy?

First of all, essential changes took place in the markets. Thanks to price liberalization and the control of the supply of credit the so-called seller's market, a typical feature of communist economy, has been eliminated, and shortages of goods were substantially reduced, that is, the condition of permanent suppressed inflation has been abolished. Simultaneously the buyer's market has gradually evolved. As a result virtually all enterprises for the first time in their existence have faced a demand constraint.

The socialized sector, which in 1989 still produced 80.8 per cent of the national income, reduced its demand for bank credit by three forms of adjustment behaviour. First, state-owned enterprises reduced the level of output. In 1990, the volume of output produced by the socialized industry was 25 per cent lower than in 1989. Second, state-owned enterprises reduced their demand for bank credit for working capital by the rise of claims against themselves, that is, by creating trade credit, as in the previous decade. This credit compensated for the difficulties arising from high interest rates on bad credit from the use of credit ceilings and from problems with selling manufactured goods. During the entire first half of 1990 the value of creditor resulting from deliveries was above 52 per cent of the enterprises' current assets. A third way to diminish the need for working capital credits was the attempt to issue securities by enterprises, particularly bills of exchange. At the end of 1989 the National Bank of Poland committed itself to rediscount these bills, assuming that in this way it would control the substitution of trade credit for bank credit, and thus would be capable of more precise management of the money supply. Until now, however, bills of exchange have not gained much in popularity. They still have not become a basic instrument in the enterprises' payments mechanism. This is due mainly to the fact that their issue is linked to civil responsibility and the ease to using trade credit outside the control of the banking system. Other types of securities, which could be used to finance the workings of enterprises in 1990, have also not played a major role. This was a direct result of the non-existence of financial markets.

A paradoxical situation emerged as a result of all these processes. The socialized sector has gone into a deep recession and has generated rising unemployment, while simultaneously the average financial situation of enterprises comprising it improved, and bankruptcies were virtually non-existent. This improvement in the financial situation was mainly due to much higher than expected price rises, which in turn were the result of the monopolistic power of state-owned enterprise and the problems of the money supply control resolved above. Thus, despite very tight credit (and fiscal) policies as well as nearly absolute domestic economic liberalization, allocative mechanisms have not appeared and the structure of this basic sector of Polish economy practically has not began to change.

As the private sector is not monopolized, and it does not create "chains of insolvency" as the socialized sector does, the policy of strict credit control forced different types of adjustment attitudes, particularly in the private sector outside agriculture. In the first quarter of 1990 more small businesses were closed down or temporarily ceased functioning than new entities were created. Nonetheless, in subsequent months the small business sector began to expand, mainly in trade and service activities.

Bankruptcies have not taken place in the private farming sector. However, as in the remaining sectors, farmers also tried to reduce the output as evidenced by their lower demand for agricultural means of production, which was to a great extent a result of the policy of high interest rates. Thus, the processes of selection and restructuring, which were expected to be the result of the full liberalization of the economy and tight economic policy, have taken place only in part of the private sector.

While interpreting the above described phenomena from the point of view of the financial system, it is necessary to point out that the distorted results of the monetary policy were intensified by a quick and nearly absolute cut in budget subsidies. It is understandable that this had to be done to restore a correct system of relative prices and to hamper hyperinflation. On the other hand, due to the rigidities of the financial system and its great simplicity, the sudden withdrawal from wide budget subsidies combined with non-selective tight credit policy led to huge negative side-effects, for example, in the field of housing, where prices jumped and long-term recessionary tendencies substantially deepened.

In consequence of a much larger drop in output, rapidly increasing unemployment, and stronger persistence of inflation than expected, macroeconomic policy has undergone a certain gradual evolution. Already in mid March 1990 some selectivity concerning agricultural credit policy was restored. In the second half of the year a policy of preferential credit was widened to other parts of the private sector, mainly newly created private businesses. Since mid 1990, a yearly based interest rate on bank credits was restored. Not only did credit policy become less tight but also budget expenses increased and incomes policy was loosened. Attempts were also made to prepare more coherent policy packets concerning two sectors of the economy: housing and farming. The works on privatization were also somewhat accelerated.

As a result of these changes, especially in credit and incomes policy, the new private sector began to develop quicker, the farming sector managed to harvest its crop without major problems, and real wages in the socialized sector stopped to go down. Nevertheless, recession in the latter sector has not ended. Simultaneously, since the end of August, inflationary pressure has re-intensified.

This rise of inflation encouraged a new tightening of monetary policy:

in October and November interest rates and reserve requirement ratios were once again increased. There was concern, confirmed by the 1991 economic processes, that these changes would not help in the recovery of the Polish economy. These dilemmas, however, confirm the existence of the inconsistency between the financial system, economic policy, and development by the fact that under the existing institutional circumstances a non-inflationary economic growth is not possible.

6.5 THE LESSONS

The 1990 experience in Poland has fully shown a collision between the need for quick stabilization and the present anachronistic financial system. The adoption of an orthodox programme, that is, implying a perfect spillover of monetary flows throughout the economy and a full responsiveness of economic agents to variables of monetary and fiscal policies, led to highly distorted effects. Macroeconomic policies aimed at financial discipline applied to a rigid financial system induced a major recession, which did not stimulate greater changes in the structure of the economy, without definitely hampering inflation.

The Polish 1990 experiences support research stressing that neo-classical economics cannot properly underpin reforms in post-Communist economies. Then, if there is no hyperinflation, orthodox (that is, essentially based on neoclassical assumptions) programmes should not be the leading element of economic policy in the transition process.

The main lesson from the Polish 1990 experience is the conclusion that countries which embarked on the transition process (and which do not have hyperinflationary pressures) should in the first instance pay more attention to institutional changes and adopt more selective macropolicies. The former means that the buildup of the market economy infra-structure should be accelerated, mainly the development of the financial system. The abolition of selective credit and fiscal policies in the situation of a primitive financial system, that is, the existing rigidities and non-existence of smooth transmission mechanisms, hampers the structural changes by reducing the scale of selective processes.

However, the buildup of the market economy infra-structure cannot be accelerated beyond a certain point. This is due to the fact that the creation of a new institutional framework is strictly linked – among other things – to the privatization of the economy, the demonopolization of the socialized sector, and the learning process of the economic agents. A new institutional framework does not only mean a new legal framework and a change in the quantity of institutions (for example, in a number of banks). A new institutional framework means also, if not mainly, a rise in the quality of services performed by the economic institutions, that is, a change in the behaviour of these institutions.

While economic policy can be diametrically changed overnight, institutional development by its nature has a gradual, evolving, character. As a consequence of this evolutionary character of institutional buildup, the principles of the current economic policy should be linked to these gradual modifications. In order to minimize the costs of transition from a bureaucratic coordination mechanism to a market one, the construction of economic policy has to be strictly linked to the progress in the institutional buildup of the economy.

The current economic discussion about the future of post-Communist societies shows a complete rejection of a concept of the so-called "Third Way". In light of the experiences of the last twenty years, this concept of a blend of best features of a market and Communist economies is another Utopian system which belongs to the history of economic thought. However, the concept of a third way understood as a way to move to a market economy from a command economy is still well-founded. Post-Communist countries can neither rely on market experiments performed by some former Communist governments, which led to great destabilization, nor should they – as the Polish case shows – rely on orthodox programmes based on neo-classical paradigms. Because of the existing social and economic differences among post-Communist countries, their governments have to work out their own visions of how to reach the market system. In this sense the concept of a third way (more exactly speaking: of several third ways) continues to be present.

NOTES

1. See for instance Schumpeter (1934), Gurley and Shaw (1960) and Fry (1988).
2. Gurley and Shaw (1960).
3. Kornai (1990).
4. For convenience I will use the expression "state-owned enterprises" interchangeably with "enterprises from socialized sector" and "socialized enterprises" (the last two terms also include cooperative enterprises).
5. In practice, however, they often included quite sizeable foreign assets (e.g. private foreign currency accounts) as well as illicit assets (e.g., trade credit which developed between socialized enterprises).
6. There were, however, major changes in the investment financing. In the early stage of a communist economy they were usually financed by budget subsidies. Later, bank credits acquired more importance in this respect.
7. Podolski (1973).
8. Kornai (1980), Topinski (1989).
9. Beksiak and Libura (1969).
10. For a more detailed information on the financial systems in communist economies in the 1980s, see *Financial Reform in Socialist Economies* (1969).
11. Schumpeter (1939), Gurley and Shaw (1960).
12. Suppressed inflation is linked to the existence of adminstered prices, thus the proportions between open and suppressed inflation may vary.
13. Kornai (1990).
14. See Polanski (1989).
15. On the quantitative development of the Polish banking sector see Table 8 in the Statistical Appendix.
16. The links between the modifications in the monetary system, changes in economic policy, and the inflation in Poland in the 1980s are described in detail in Polanski (1991).
17. See tables 1 and 2 in the Appendix. It is necessary, however, to stress that some structural changes took place that year: while the volume of output in the socialized sector dropped by 2.6%, private sector output rose by 12%.
18. On the political and social circumstances leading to the adoption of this programme see Kaminski (1990).
19. Dabrowski (1990).
20. The adoption of incomes policy was the only important non-orthodox measure in this programme.
21. See Tables 3 and 6.
22. See Table 7.
23. The dynamics of the rise of the money supply during 1990 is shown in Table 4.
24. Other instruments of monetary control used by the Polish central bank were the interest rate on refinance credit and the rediscount rate on bills of exchange. Their evolution is shown in Table 6. Both of them in the situation of banks'

115

excess liquidity (due to the above mentioned trade surplus), and enterprises reluctance to use bills of exchange, did not play major effective role in controlling the money supply. Also remaining monetary instruments were of very minor (as in the case of attempts to conduct money market operations) or even none (as in the case of lombard credit mechanism) importance.

25. For more information on these processes see Tables 4 and 5.

26. Another important factor which influenced the decline of farming demand for means of production was the inconvenient relation between their prices and the prices of agricultural output.

27. Murrell (1991).

STATISTICAL APPENDIX*

Table 1: Gross National Income (GNI) in Poland, 1979-1990
(Constant prices, percentage change)[1]

Year	GNI Manufactured	GNI Distributed	GNI Distributed per capita
1979-1982[2]	−5.4	−6.6	−7.4
1983-1987[2]	4.3	4.2	3.4
1988	4.7	4.6	4.0
1989	0.1	0.3	0.0
1990	−13.4	−18.2	−18.5

1. Material Product System.
2. Average.
Sources: Polish Central Statistical Office Yearbooks.

*This was prepared by Dr, Polanski except Table 7, which was prepared by the authors of Chapter 5.

Table 2: Inflation in Poland, 1979-1989 (Percentage change)

Year	GNI Distributed Deflator	Food Retail Prices State Shops	Private Shops
1979-1981[1]	10.6	11.0	29.0
1982-1987[1]	32.1	32.6	23.1
1988	69.3	48.3	56.8
1989	294.4	337.7	278.6

1. Average.
Source: Polish Central Statistical Office Yearbooks.

Table 3: Inflation and Wages in the Socialized and Private Sectors in Poland, 1990 (Percentage change from previous month unless indicated otherwise)

Month	Consumer Retail Prices	Nominal Wages	Real Wages	Real Wages[1]
January	79.6	1.8	-43.1	-43.3
February	23.8	15.4	-6.8	-47.2
March	4.3	40.1	34.3	-29.0
April	7.5	-8.8	-15.2	-39.8
May	4.6	-3.8	-8.0	-44.6
June	3.4	1.4	-1.9	-45.7
July	3.6	10.8	6.9	-41.9
August	1.8	4.8	2.9	-40.2
September	4.6	7.9	3.2	-38.3
October	5.7	13.6	7.5	-33.7
November	4.9	13.0	7.7	-28.6
December	5.9	9.6	3.5	-26.1
Dec. 1990 to Dec.1989	249.3	158.1	-26.1	

1. Cumulative changes from December of previous year.
Source: Polish Central Statistical Office.

117

Table 4: Socialized Industry Output (Constant prices) and Money Supply (M2) in Poland, 1990 (Percentage change from previous month unless indicated otherwise)

Month	Output	Output[1]	M2	M2[1]
January	−19.3	-19.3	41.5	41.5
February	−14.2	-30.7	21.6	72.1
March	10.5	-23.5	21.6	109.3
April	-8.5	-30.0	14.4	139.5
May	4.1	-27.1	11.6	167.3
June	-0.2	-27.3	13.7	204.0
July	-4.8	-30.8	14.2	247.0
August	7.7	-25.4	12.5	290.4
September	0.3	-25.2	7.4	319.2
October	11.7	-16.4	6.7	347.2
November	-3.4	-19.3	7.2	379.6
December	-5.8	-23.9	2.1	389.6
Dec. 1990 to Dec. 1989	-23.9		389.6	

Note: M2 foreign currency deposits excluded.
1. Cumulative changes from December 1989.
Source: Polish Central Statistical Office and National Bank of Poland.

Table 5: Unemployment in Poland, 1990 (In %)

Month	Of Total Workforce	Of Total Workforce Agriculture Excluded
January	0.3	0.4
March	1.5	2.0
July	3.8	5.2
December	6.1	8.3

Source: Polish Central Statistical Office.

Table 6: Interest Rate on Refinance Credit and the Rediscount Rate
by the National Bank of Poland, 1990

Month	Interest Rate	Rediscount Rate
January	36.0	14.2
February	20.0	7.4
March	10.0	5.1
April	8.0	4.2
May	5.5	2.9
June	4.0	2.3
July-September	2.5	2.1
October	3.0	2.6
November-December	3.7	3.3

Note: Between January and June the interest rate was published on a monthly basis, while the rediscount rate was expressed on a quarterly one; since July both rates have been published on a yearly basis. All data in the table are shown on a monthly basis.
Source: National Bank of Poland.

Table 7: Reserve Requirement Ratios in Poland, 1989-1990 (In %)

Type of Accounts	1989			1990		
	1.03	1.03	1.04	1.08	15.10	1.12
Transaction	15	9	15	27	30	30
Saving	10	9	15	17	20	30
Time	5	9	15	7	8	10

Source: National Bank of Poland.

Table 8: Development of the Banking System in Poland, 1986-1990

Item	1986	1987	1988	1989	1990
Total Number	4	5	7	20	50
State Banks[1]	4	5	6	16	16
Non-Treasury Corporate Banks[2]			1	4	33
Foreign Banks[3]					1

Notes:
(a) The entries in the table show the number of operating banks at the end of the year. (b) The 1662 cooperative banks linked to the Agricultural Bank (BGZ), which were nominally independent units but in fact simply branches, are counted as 1 bank for the purpose of this table. It must be stressed, however, that in 1990 85 cooperative banks left the Agricultural Bank planning to begin independent activity. (c) At the end of 1990 there were 18 banks that obtained licence to operate but still were under organization.

1. Including state-owned corporations.
2. Banks in form of corporations whose shares do not belong mainly to the State Treasury, and new private banks.
3. Corporations with more than 51% of foreign capital.

Source: National Bank of Poland.

Table 7: Polish Interest Rates in 1991

	Date of auction	Refinancing credit interest %	Yield on Treasury Bills /with income tax correction/ average discount rate %	max discount rate %
NRP bills 28 days	7.03	72	85.34	88.82
	14.03	72	86.03	86.96
	21.03	72	85.34	86.03
	28.03	72	82.79	83.49
	4.04	72	77.49	78.64
	11.04	72	75.42	77.03
	18.04	72	77.03	83.95
	25.04	72	77.26	82.33
	30.04	72	–	–
NRP bills 91 days	7.03	72	87.36	87.36
	14.03	72	86.69	87.36
	21.03	72	87.19	87.36
	28.03	72	86.10	86.10
	4.04	72	84.33	85.68
	11.04	72	81.41	83.16
	18.04	72	81.07	85.26
	25.04	72	80.30	80.33
	30.04	72	–	–
	9.05	59	58.11	58.35
	16.05	59	58.27	58.27
	23.05	59	58.11	58.11
	29.05	59	–	–
	6.06	59	58.27	58.27
	13.06	59	61.17	61.25
BRP bills 182 days	6.06	59	58.31	58.31
Treasury bills 4 weeks	5.05	59	65.14	70.15
	13.05	59	67.64	70.15
	20.05	59	67.64	70.15
	27.05	59	67.64	69.69
	3.06	59	68.10	69.01
	10.06	59	67.64	68.32
Treasury bills 8 weeks	13.05	59	62.96	71.79
	20.05	59	68.37	70.33
	27.05	59	69.60	69.60
	3.06	59	71.92	71.92
	10.06	59	70.94	71.64

Note the refinancing credit cut rate always exceeded the discount rate except 9 May – 6 June, on issues with a maturity over 90 days.

Bibliography

Akerlof, G.A. et al (1991) 'East Germany in from the Cold: the Economic Aftermath of Currency Reform', *Brookings Papers on Economic Activity*, no.1, pp.1–105.

Autorenkollektiv (1979) *Lexikon der Wirtschaft* (3rd edn), Verlag Die Wirtschaft, East Berlin.

Autorenkollektiv (1979–1980) *Ökonomisches Lexikon*, Verlag Die Wirtschaft, East Berlin, 3 vols.

Autorenkollektiv (1981) *Sozialistische Finanzwirtschaft*, Verlag Die Wirtschaft, East Berlin.

Bácskai, T. (1989) "The reorganisation of the Banking System", *Eastern European Economics*, vol.28, pp.79–92.

Bank (1980) *Monetary Control: A Consultation Paper by H.M. Treasury and the Bank of England*, HMSO. Cmnd 7858, London.

Beksiak, J. and Libura, U. (1969) *Równowaga gospodarcza w socjalizmie* (Economic equilibrium under socialism), Parístwowe Wydawnictwo Ekonomiczne, Warsaw.

Belassa, B. (1989) "Next steps in the Hungarian Economic Reform", *Eastern European Economics*, vol.28, part 1, pp.34–53.

Bolz, K. (1985) 'Wahrung/Wahrungspolitik' in H. Zimmermann (1985), 2, pp.1449–1456.

Brabant, J.M. (1990) "Socialist Economics: The disequilibrium school and the shortage economy", *Journal of Economic Perspectives*, vol.4, no.2., pp.135–177

Buck, H–J. (1976) 'Finanzierungssystem der DDR' in Büschgen (ed.) (1970), pp.253–271.

Buck, H–J. (1985a) 'Finanzsystem' in Zimmermann (1985), vol.1, pp.400–411.

Buck, H–J. (1985b) 'Geldtheorie und Geldpolitik' in Zimmermann (1985), vol.1, pp.487–509.

Buck, H–J. (1985c) 'Zins und Zinspolitik' in Zimmermann (1985), vol.2, pp.1543–1551.

Bundesministerium für innerdeutsche Beziehungen (1987), *Materialien zum Bericht zur Lage der Nation im geteilten Deutschland 1987,* Bundesministerium für innerdeutsche Beziehungen, Bonn.

Büschgen, L. (ed.) (1970) *Handwörterbuch der Finanzwissenschaft,* C.E. Poeschel, Stuttgart.

Collier, I.L. (1983) 'The Estimation of the Gross Domestic Product and Its Growth Rate for the German Democratic Republic', *World Bank Staff Working Papers Number 773,* World Bank, Washington, D.C.

Collier, I.L. and Siebert, (1991) 'The Economic Integration of Post–Wall Germany', *American Economic Review,* Papers and Proceedings, pp.196–201.

Cornelsen, D. (1989a) 'Survey' in German Institute for Economic Research (1989), pp.3–8.

Cornelsen, D. (1989b) 'The GDR in the 1980s' in German Institute for Economic Research (1989), pp.9–17.

Cornelsen, D. (1989c) 'Die Volkswirtschaft der DDR: Wirtschaftssystem – Entwicklung – Probleme', in Weidenfeld and Zimmermann (1989), pp.258–275.

Cornelsen, D. et al (1989) 'The GDR System at the Beginning of the 1980s: Reform in Small Stages' in German Institute for Economic Research (1987), pp.43–48.

Crnkovic, R. Hanzekovic, M. and Ott, K. (1981) *Problemi jugoslavenskog bankovnog sistema* (Problems of the Yugolsav Financial System), Institute of Public Finance, Zagreb.

Dabrowski, M. (1990) 'Trzeba jeszce wytrwab' (One has to be persistent), *Polityka,* Warsaw.

Dawson, G. (1992) *The Cost of Unemployment and Inflation,* Edward Elgar, Aldershot.

Deckers, J. (1974) *Die Transformation des Bankensystems in der sowjetischen Besatzungszone/DDR von 1945 bis 1952,* Wirtschaftswissenschaftliche Veröffentlichungen des Osteuropa– Instituts an der Freien Universität Berlin, Band 38, Duncker und Humblot, Berlin.

Deutsches Institut für Wirtschaftsforschung Berlin (1984) *Handbuch DDR–Wirtschaft* 4th edn, Rowohlt, Reinbek bei Hamburg.

Deutsches Institut für Wirtschaftsforschung Berlin (1990), *DDR – Wirtschaft im Umbruch,* Deutsches Institut für Wirtschaftsforschung, Berlin.

Economic Bulletin, (1986) 'The GDR economy at the end of the Five–Year Plan, 1981/85', vol.23, no.2, pp.4–14.

Economic Bulletin, (1989a) 'The GDR Economy at the Start of 1989', vol.26, no.2, pp.4–10.

Economic Bulletin, (1989b) 'The GDR Economy in the First Half of 1989', vol.26, no.9, pp.4–8.

Economic Bulletin, (1990a) 'The East German Economy at the Start of 1990', vol.27, no.2, pp.1–3.

Economic Bulletin, (1990b) 'Quantitative Aspects of Economic and Financial Reform in the GDR', vol.27, no.5, pp.1–19.

Economic Bulletin, (1990c) 'The World Economy and the West German Economy in the Autumn of 1990', vol.27, no.10, pp.1–24.

Economic Bulletin, (1991) 'Economic Trends in 1991/92', vol.28, no.7, pp.1–25.

Fischer, A. (1975) *Sowjetische Deutschlandspolitik im zweiten Weltkrieg*, Deutsche Verlags–Anstalt, Stuttgart.

Friedman, M. (1977) *Inflation and Unemployment*, Institute of Economic Affairs, London.

Fry, Maxwell J. (1988) *Money, Interest and Banking in Economic Development*, John Hopkins Press, Baltimore.

Fry, Maxwell J. (1989) "Financial Development: Theories and Recent Experiences", in *Oxford Review of Economic Policy*, vol.5, no.4, (Winter), pp.13–28.

Gaspari, M. (1988) 'Neki otvoreni problemi finansijskog i centralnobankarskog sistema i monetarne politike in Jugoslaviji (Some open problems of the financial, central banking system and monetary policy in Yugoslavia), *Jugoslovensko bankastro*, vol.9, pp.5–18.

Garvy, G. (1966) *Money, Banking and Credit in Eastern Europe*, Federal Reserve Bank of New York, New York.

Gerloff, W. and Neumark, F. (eds.) (1958) *Handbuch der Finanzwissenschaft*, Berlin.

German Institute for Economic Research (1989), *GDR and Eastern Europe – A Handbook*, Avebury, Aldershot.

Gowland, D.H. (1982) *Monetary Control in Theory and Practice*, Routledge, London. (2nd edn, 1984).

Gowland, D.H. (1990) *Understanding Macroeconomics*, Edward Elgar, Aldershot.

Grubic, S. (1990) *Banke u Jugoslavije u 1990* (Banks in Yugolslavia in 1990), a special edition of Ekonomska, Belgrade.

Gurtz, J. and Kaltofen, G. (1982) *Der Staatshaushalt der DDR* (2nd edn), Verlag Die Wirtschaft, East Berlin .

Gutmann, G. (ed.) (1983) *Basisbereiche der Wirtschaftspolitik in der DDR. Geld–, Finanz– und Preispolitik*, Verlag Meyn, Asperg bei Stuttgart.

Haase, H.A, (1982) 'Deutsche Demokratische Republik' in Neumark (1982), vol.4, pp.543–575.

Haase, H.A. (1985a) 'Bankwesen', in Zimmermann (1985), vol.1, pp.143–148.

Haase, H.A. (1985b) 'Staatshaushalt', in Zimmermann (1985.), vol.2, pp1280–1296.

Haase, H.A. (1985c) ' Steuern', in Zimmermann (1985.), vol.2, pp.1311–1331.

Haffner, F. (1987) 'Monet re Zentralplanung und Volkswirtschaftsplanung' in Thieme (1987).

Hahmann, H-H. (ed.) (1982) *The Eastern European Economics in the 1970s*, Butterworth, London.

Hamel, H. (ed.) (1983) *Bundesrepublik Deutschland – DDR. Die Wirtschaftssysteme* (4th edn), C.H. Beck, Munich,.

Hamel, H. (1983a) 'Ordnungspolitische Gestaltung der Wirtschaftssysteme' in Hamel (1983).

Hare, P.G. (1989) "Economic Development in Eastern Europe, A Review Article", *Oxford Economic Papers*, vol.41, no.4, pp.672–698.

Hare, P.G. (1990) "From Central Planning to market economy – some microeconomic issues", *Economic Journal*, vol.100 (June), pp.581–595.

Hartwig, K–H. and Thieme, H.J. (1985) 'Monetary Goals, Targets and Indicators in Centrally–Planned Economies: the Example of the German Democratic Republic', *Jahrbuch der Wirtschaft Osteuropas*, vol.11, no.1, pp.173–186.

Haustein, H–D. (1989) 'Role and Functioning of Industrial Enterprises in the German Democratic Republic' in United Nations (1989), pp.103–108.

Hayek, F.A. (1972) *A Tiger by the Tail*, Hobart Paperback, no.4, IEA, London.

Hedtkamp, G. (1965) 'Finanzwirtschaft der sowjetischen Besatzungszone' *Handwörterbuch der Sozialwissenschaften*, J.C.B Mohr &c., Stuttgart &c., vol.12, pp.585–591.

Hedtkamp, G. (1987) 'Die öffentliche Finanzwirtschaft als Systemelement' in Bundesministerium für innerdeutsche Beziehungen (1987), pp.192–204.

Horuchi A. (1984) "The 'low interest rate policy' and economic growth in post-war Japan", *Developing Countries*, vol.22, no.4, pp.243–258.

Hungarian Chamber of Commerce (1990) "Hungaropress", *Economic Information*, vols.6–12, 1990.

Hungarian Trade Journal (1990) September, vol.40, no.9.

Kahler, G. (1989) 'Economic and Social Development Aims in the German Democratic Republic' in United Nations (1989), pp.176–182.

Kaemmel, E. (1958) 'Das Finanzsystem der Deutschen Demokratischen Republik' in Gerloff and Neumark (eds.), 1958, vol.3, pp.396–419.

Kaminski, B. (1990) "Systematic Underpinnings of the Transition in Poland: The Shadow of the Roundtable Agreement". Paper presented at Conference "Politics and Economics of the Transition Tubingen", October 10–14, 1990.

Kerm, D. (1990) "The Risk of Change", *Banking World*, vol.8, no.4, p.3.

Kessides, C., King, T., Nuti, M. and Sokil, C. (1989) *Financial Reform in Socialist Economics*, The World Bank, Washington D.C.

Keynes (1923) *A Tract on Monetary Reform* reprinted in Keynes (1971), vol.VII.

Keynes (1936) *The General Theory of Employment, Interest and Money*, Macmillan, also vol.XIV of his collected works (Keynes 1971).

Keynes, J.M. (1971) *Collected Writings*, Macmillan for the Royal Society, London.

Knauff, R. (1983) 'Die Funktionsmechanismen der Wirtschaftssysteme' in Hamel (1988), pp.116–198.

Kornai, J. (1980) *Economics of Shortage*, Amsterdam, North Holland.

Kornai, J. (1986a) 'The Hungarian Reform Process: Visions, Hopes and Reality', *Journal of Economic Literature*, vol.XXIV, p.1687, (Dec).

Kornai, J. (1986b) "The Soft Budget Constraint", *Kyklos,* vol.39, Facs I.

Kornai, J. (1990) "The affinity between ownership forms and co–ordination mechanisms. The common experience of reform in socialist countries, *Journal of Economic Perspectives,* vol.4, no.3, pp.131–147.

Lacker, J.M. (1991) "Why is There Debt?", *Economic Review,* Federal Reserve Bank of Richmond, vol.77/4, (July/Aug) pp.3–19.

Leptin, G. (1977) *Die öffentliche Haushalt der DDR, Berichte des Bundesinstituts für ostwissenschaftliche und internationale Studien,* Bundesinstitut &c. Cologne, vol.3.

Levchuk, I. (1979) 'Money Circulation and the Role of Money under Socialism' in *Problems of Economics,* vol.22, pp.71–87.

Lipschitz, L. (1990) 'Introduction and Overview' in Lipschitz and McDonald (eds) (1990), pp.1–16.

Lipschitz, L. and McDonald, D. (eds) (1990) *German Unification. Economic Issues,* International Monetary Fund, Washington, D.C.

Marer, P. (1983) *Evaluation and Estimation of National Accounts Statistics of Centrally Planned Economies,* World Bank, Washington, D.C.

Mayer T. (ed.) (1978) *The Structure of Monetarism,* Norton.

Mayer, T. (1990) 'The Role of Fiscal and Structural Policies in German Unification' in Lipschitz and McDonald (1990), pp.165–171.

Mayer, T. and Thumann, G. (1990) 'German Democratic Republic: Background and Plans for Reform' in Lipschitz and McDonald (1990), pp.49–70.

McKinnon, R.I. (1989) "Financial Liberalization and Economic Development: A Reassessment of interest rate policies in Asia and Latin America", *Oxford Review of Economic Policy,* vol.5, no.4, (Winter), pp.29–54.

Melzer, M. (1982) 'The GDR – Economic Policy Caught between Pressure for Efficiency and Lack of Ideas' in Hahmann (1982), pp.45–90.

Melzer, M. (1985) 'Preissystem und Preispolitik' in Zimmermann (ed.) (1985), vol.2, pp.1032–1044.

Melzer, M. (1987) 'The New Planning and Steering Mechanisms in the GDR – Between Pressure for Efficiency and Success' in 'Intensification Policy', *Studies in Comparative Communism,* vol.20, no.1.

Melzer, M. (1989) 'Price Formation' in German Institute for Economic Research, (1989) pp.49–54.

Melzer, M. and Stahnke, A.A. (1986) 'The GDR Faces the Dilemmas of the 1980s: Caught between the Need for New Methods and Restricted Options' in United States Congress (1986), vol.3: Country Studies on Eastern Europe and Yugoslavia, United States GPO, Washington, D.C., pp.131–168.

Ministry of Finance, Warsaw (1989) *Letter of Intent*, Ministry of Finance, Warsaw.

Mohieldin, M. (1991) *On Financial Liberalization in Developing Countries*, Mimeo, University of Warwick.

Murrell, P. (1991) 'Can Neoclassical Economics Underpin the Economic Reform of Centrally Planned Economics', *Journal of Economic Perspectives*, vol.X, p.7.

Musgrave, R.A. (1969) *Fiscal Systems*, Greenwood Press, Westport. Conn.

Neave, E.H. (1991) *The Economic Organization of a Financial System*, Routledge, London.

Nettl, J.P. (1977) The Eastern Zone and Soviet Policy in Eastern Germany, 1945–1950, Oxford University Press, London.

Neumark, F. (1982) (ed.) *Handbuch der Finanzwissenschaft*, 3rd edn, J.C.B. Mohr, Tübingen.

Ott, K. (1988) *The Yugoslav Banking System*, Institute of Public Finance, Zagreb.

Ott, K. (1989) 'O nekim pitanjuna odnosa a drzavom i neovisnosti Narodna Banke' (Some Questions Concerning Relations with the Government and Independence of the National Bank), *Teorijskle i practicini problemi financijskog sistema Jugoslavije*, Institute of Public Finance, Zagreb.

Pagano and Roell (1992) "Auction Markets, Dealership Markets and Execution Risk", *European Economic Review*, forthcoming.

Phillips, A.L. (1986) *Soviet Policy towards East Germany Reconsidered. The Postwar Decade*, Greenwood Press, New York.

Podolski, T.M. (1973) *Socialist Banking and Monetary Control: The Experience of Poland*, Cambridge University Press, Cambridge.

Polanski, Z. (1989) 'Dylematy polityki antyinflacyjnej u progu lat dziewirbdziesi tych' (The dilammas surraounding an anti-inflationary policy for the early 1990s), *Bank i Kredyt*, nos.8–9, pp.20–24, Warsaw.

Polanski, Z. (1991) 'Inflation and the Monetary System in Poland in the 1980s', *Osteuropa Wirtschaft*, forthcoming.

Pöhl, R. (ed.), (1977) *Handbook of the Economy of the German Democratic Republic*, Saxon House, Farnborough.

Prindl, A. (1990) "A Bankers View", *Banking World*, vol.8, no.4, p.27.

Rogic, Z. (1990) 'Moetarno – kredit na politika' (Money – Credit Policy) in *Aktualni pronblemi privrednih Kretanja i ekonomske politke Jugoslavije*, Institute of Economics, Zagrab.

Rytlewski, R. (1985) 'Wirtschaft' in Zimmermann (1985), pp.1032–1044.

Sandford, G.W. (1983) *From Hitler to Ulbricht. The Communist Reconstruction of East Germany, 1945–1946*, Princeton U.P., Princeton N.J.

Schilar, H. (1989) 'Planned Economy in the German Democratic Republic – Foundations and Changes' in United Nations (1984), pp.28–33.

Schinasi, G.J. et al (1990) 'Monetary and Financial Issues in German Unification' in Lipschitz and McDonald (1990), pp.144–154.

Schnitzer, M. (1972) *East and West Germany: a Comparative Economic Analysis*, Praeger, New York.

Schumpeter, J.A. (1934) *The Theory of Economic Development*, Harvard University Press, Cambridge.

Schwartau, C. and Vortm ᵢ. (1989) 'Die materiellen Lebensbedingungen in der DDR' in Weidenfeld and Zimmermann (1989), pp.292–307.

Shone, R. (1984) *Issues in Macroeconomics*, Martin Robertson, Oxford.

Siebert, H. (1991) 'German Unification: the Economics of Transition', *Economic Policy*, vol.13, pp.287–340.

Sinclair, P. (1987) *Unemployment*, Basil Blackwell, Oxford.

Sokil, C.M. (1980) "Hungarian Financial and Labour Market Reforms", *Eastern European Economics*, vol.28, part 1, pp.53–64.

Staatliche Zentralverwaltung für Statistik (1956–1989) *Statistisches Jahrbuch der Deutschen Demokratischen Republik*, Staatsverlag der DDR, East Berlin.

Statistisches Bundesamt (1990) *DDR 1990 – Zahlen und Fakten*, Statistisches Bundesamt, Bonn.

Stiglitz, J.E. (1989) "Financial Markets and Development", *Oxford Review of Economic Policy*, vol.5, no.4, (Winter), pp.55–68.

Tardós, M. (1989) "Can Hungary's Monetary Policy Succeed?", *Eastern European Economics*, Autumn 1989, vol.28, part 1, pp.64–79.

Thalheim et al (1987) 'Das Leitbild der "sozialistischen Planwirtschaft"' in Bundesministerium für innerdeutsche Beziehungen (1987), pp.96–110.

Thalheim, K.C. (1987) Entstehung und Entwicklung des Wirtschaftssystems der DDR' in Bundesministerium für innerdeutsche Beziehungen (1987), pp.17–25.

Thieme, H.J. (1983) 'Gesamtwirtschaftliche Instabilit ten: Erscheinungsformen, Ursachen und Konzepte ihrer Bekmpfung' in Hamel (ed.) (1983), pp.262–337.

Thieme, H.J. (1987) (ed.), *Geldtheorie. Entwicklung, Stand und systemvergleichende Anwendung*, Monographien der List Gesellschaft e.V., Neue Folge, Band 8, Nomos Verlag, Baden–Baden.

Thieme, H.J. (1987a) 'Geld und Kredit in beiden Wirtschaftssystemen' in Bundesministerium für innerdeutsche Beziehungen (1987), pp.182–191.

Thieme, H.J. (1987b) 'Produktions– und Besch ftigungseffekte monet rer Impulse in sozialistischen Planwirtschaften' in H.J. Thieme (1987), pp.295–318.

Thumann, G. (1990) 'The System of Public Finance in the German Democratic Republic and the Challenges of Fiscal Reform' in Lipschitz and McDonald (1990), pp.155–164.

Topinski, A (1989) *Inflacja a funkcjonwanie gospodarki polskiej* (Inflation and the functioning of the Polish Economy), Parístwowe Wydawnictwo Ekonomiczne, Warsaw.

United Nations (Economic Commission for Europe) (1989), 'Economic Reforms in the European Centrally Planned Economies', *Economic Studies*, no.1, United Nations, New York.

128

United States Congress (1986) Joint Economic Committee *East European Economics: slow growth in the 1980s Vol.3: Country Studies in Eastern Europe and Yugoslavia*, United States GPO, Washington D.C.

Vortmann, H. 'Social Security' in German Institute for Economic Research, (1989) pp.153–158.

Vortmann, H. 'The State Budget' in German Institute for Economic Research, (1989) pp.145–151.

Weidenfeld, W. and Zimmermann, H. (eds), (1989) *Deutschland–Handbuch. Eine doppelte Bilanz 1949–1989*, Bundeszentrale für politische Bildung, Bonn.

Wilczynski, J. (1981) *An Encyclopaedic Dictionary of Marxism, Socialism and Communism*, Macmillan, London.

Wilkens, H. (1981) *The Two German Economies*, Gower Publishing, Farnborough.

Williamson, O. (1988) "Corporate Finance and Corporate Governance", *Journal of Finance*, vol.43, pp.567–91.

Yugoslavia (1989) *Financial Restructuring Policies and Priorities*, I.II, World Bank, Washington D.C.

Zimmermann, H. (1985) (ed.), *DDR–Handbuch,* Verlag Wissenschaft und Politik, Cologne, 2 vols.

DATA SOURCES

Poland

National Bank of Poland. Various publications
Polish Central Statistical Office. Various publications

Yugoslavia

Bulletins of the National Bank of Yugoslavia
Monthly Review of Economic Statistics of the SFRY
Sluzbeni listovi SFRJ (Official Gazettes SFRY)
Statistical Yearbook of Yugoslavia

Index

131

6, 17
banking system 27–28, 33–35
and financial planning 22–25,
    31–33
and the financial system 16–21
monetary policy 35–36
pricing system 28–30, 36–37
German Economic Monetary and
    Social Union (GEMSU), 17, 39–43
German Note Issue Bank (DNB) 19,
    27–28
German Foreign Trade Bank 27
Girozentrale and Händerbank 87
Governance system 7
Government
    authority 50
    local and central 76
    spending 61

High powered money 64, 70–71
Hungary 7, 11, 13, 103
Hungarian government
    and Czech govt. 9
Hungarian industry 76, 80
Hungary's trade position 82

Import substitution 82
Industry — Infra-structure debate 87,
    112
Industry
    privately owned 9
    publicly owned 9
Inefficiency, structural 4
Inflation 30, 83, 107, 111
    arrest of 63
    costs of 5, 93
    policy 13–14
    priorities given to 11, 71
    suppressed 105
Inflationary pressure 58, 106
Institutional debate 5
institutions vs markets 5
Interest rates 83, 97, 105

on credits 95, 108, 110–111
and reserve requirements 112
subsidies 92
Inter-Governmental Conference on
    Monetary Union 14
International Monetary Fund (IMF)
    57, 108
Investment
    controls 38, 79
    and credit 81
    decisions 86
    funds 6, 104
    hunger 78–79
    income 97
Italy 76
    public sector 9

Keynes JM 5, 12
Kôhl H 13
Kornai J 7, 79, 80, 82, 105

Ligetti 84–86
Liquidity 93, 109
Liquid monetary reserves 97
Lombard credit 98–99

Macro economic policies 103, 105
    and inflation 92
    and stabilisation 11, 49–51, 106
Macroeconomic progress 17
Market
    constraints 77
    forces 10
    institutions 87, 104
    mechanism 56, 82, 89
    prices 16, 82
Market economy 38, 81, 89, 100
    transformation to 64–65, 112–113
    transition to 51, 102, 105
Marx K 5–6, 77
Mayer 12
Means of production
    ownership of 8